Barry Stratton

The hunter's handbook, containing a description of all articles required in camp

with hints on provisions and stores and receipts for camp cooking

Barry Stratton

The hunter's handbook, containing a description of all articles required in camp
with hints on provisions and stores and receipts for camp cooking

ISBN/EAN: 9783744788953

Printed in Europe, USA, Canada, Australia, Japan

Cover: Foto ©Lupo / pixelio.de

More available books at **www.hansebooks.com**

Hunter's Handbook

CONTAINING A DESCRIPTION OF

ALL ARTICLES REQUIRED IN CAMP

WITH

Hints on Provisions and Stores

AND

RECEIPTS FOR CAMP COOKING

BY

"AN OLD HUNTER"

BOSTON
LEE AND SHEPARD, PUBLISHERS
NEW YORK
CHARLES T. DILLLINGHAM
1885

Copyright, 1885,
BY LEE AND SHEPARD.

All rights reserved.

HUNTER'S HANDBOOK.

CONTENTS.

Section.		Page.
	Introduction	5
I.	Quantity of Provisions required on a Trip. and Comparative List of Provisions.	9
II.	List of Provisions from which to select.	15
III.	The Hunter's Paraphernalia	19
IV.	The Camp Fire	23
V.	General Remarks on Camp Routine	29
VI.	Cooking Utensils	39
VII.	General Remarks on Camp Cookery	45
	Index to Receipts	57
VIII.	Recipes for Camp Cookery	61
IX.	The Last Resource	111
	Index to Section X.	116
X.	On the Treatment of Drowning, Wounds, Stings, etc.,	117
	Index to Section XI.	130
XI.	Miscellaneous Receipts	131
XII.	Signs of the Weather	135

INTRODUCTION.

The want of a cheap, portable and reliable Hand Book devoted to the interior economy of the Hunter's Camp, and more especially to the Art of Camp Cookery, has long been felt. We have some excellent works on Hunting, some of which devote a few pages to these subjects, but these books, in their elaborate bindings, with their numerous illustrations, and costing a considerable sum of money, are better fitted to grace a Drawing Room table, or to occupy places in the Library, than to be carried through the vicissitudes of a campaign. Their usefulness would scarcely compensate the Hunter for the care which he would feel bound to bestow on them in order to keep their beauty unsullied by the unavoidable exposure to dampness, dirt, and the thousand little accidents of Camp life. More acceptable to the Hunter, be he professional or amateur, would be a rough and ready handbook which he could use without fear and and trembling, and which could be consigned, without compunction, to any corner of the larder, not always, in truth, dispensing the odors of Araby the Blest. Such a want I have endeavored to fill: such a is here handbook offered to the public.

Many years of experience in the economy of Camp life, supplemented by diligent research among the best authorities on the subject, have, I trust, qualified me to undertake the compilation of these pages.

The various sections of the work need not be commented on here, with the exception of Section IX, which contains the Receipts for Camp Cookery. The Receipts here given cover a large area, comprising not only the directions for preparing the frugal fare of the hardened Hunter, but also the formulas for concocting the somewhat more dainty dishes affected by the amateur Nimrod.

As to whether a professional hunter should confine himself to the commonest diet and abjure the fare of civilization, I need express no opinion. That is merely a matter of personal election. I may, however, mention the obvious fact, that the better nourished the body is, the more hardship it can endure. Good food keeps us in good health; exercise, or work, also conduces to the same desirable end. The better our health the greater pleasure do we take in working, and the greater the benefit derived therefrom. Thus we have these two powers, food and exercise, while separately benefiting us, most intimately depending on each other for their ability to bestow that benefit, and hence while undergoing plenty of exercise we must not neglect to appropriate a sufficiency of its con-comitant adjunct, nourishing food. From these facts it will be seen that the idea held by some young amateur hunters, that they should deprive themselves of their customary diet in supposed manly emulation of their more hardy professional brethren, is as hurtful as foolish. While the wiry old scout thrives on his bear meat broiled in the coals, supplemented by some meal and tea, and scorns to prepare any compound dishes, the amateur who leaves home for a week's holiday in the wilderness is liable to be seriously inconvenienced, if not actually made ill, by too great a change in his diet. Again, we must remember that to please one's self in the choice of food, as well as in other matters, is a part of that liberty which the hunter fondly expects to enjoy, and should obtain, when, casting off the shackles of civilization, he seeks pleasure, sport, and health in the wilds of the forest, or on the waters of the lagoons. Thus I have considered it to be my duty to present receipts which shall meet the desires of all classes of hunters and excursionists.

With hunters, to be able to cook their food properly, is a prime necessity of life. No more piteous object exists than the young hunter who, though surrounded by plenty, has yet to content himself with the plainest food, and that not cooked but spoiled by the injudicious application of fire. And yet there are hundreds of such amateur hunters who, when out on their initiatory shooting excursion find themselves suddenly confronted by a deficiency of which they never thought, a lamentable ignorance of the art of cooking. If such young hunters follow the advice presented in this handbook, they may expect their efforts in cooking to meet with success.

To make the work as a guide to Camp Cooking more complete, I have added some general remarks on the different modes of cooking, such as Boiling, Roasting, etc., which I hope will prove instructive.

The experience of many Trips into the wilderness has been drawn upon to present correct views to the reader, and that the pages here offered to the public will enable all hunters to escape the painful episodes which usually attend the amateur's initiation into the mysteries of Camp life is the earnest wish of

"An Old Hunter."

THE HUNTER'S HANDBOOK.

SECTION I.

THE QUANTITY OF PROVISIONS REQUIRED ON A HUNTING TRIP, AND COMPARATIVE LIST OF PROVISIONS.

In making up our list of groceries for a hunting excursion several circumstances are to be considered, the duration of the trip being, of course, the first consideration. The second consideration is as to whether we can purchase provisions *en route*. If we can, then we need not carry as much food with us as we should have to take if we were going to pass through an uninhabited country. The last consideration under which we can attempt to limit the amount of provisions which we transport, is the chance of securing the game of which we go in search. The experienced hunter can best deal with these questions himself, but while there are circumstances which may authorize him to limit to a certain extent the amount of provisions which he carries, I would most earnestly advise all amateurs to take with them enough food to provide full meals for every day of their intended stay. The inexperienced invariably carry too little food, and even when they think they are most munificently provided, they are sure to be on short commons ere they return to their homes. We may consider a few methods of arriving at an approximate idea of the quantity of provisions required by a party contemplating a hunting excursion.

If four of us start on a two-week's trip we will require, at three meals per day, enough food to provide 168 meals. This number contains only 56 dinners, and as our breakfasts and suppers are generally composed of lighter food than that which we consume at the mid-day meal, we may so far moderate our list of groceries as to provide the most substantial articles for the dinners only. I speak of confining our expenses to the lowest possible rate, as I am aware that money is very often quite a consideration even with those who can afford, for pleasure, to spend a few weeks on a hunting trip.

Another way in which to arrive at the quantity of food which we should carry, is, to consider the value thereof in money. Thus, if we pay $3, $4 or $5 per week for board we are provided with different classes of tables according to the rates which we pay. If we are willing to live on the board which $3 per week provides—very good board for a hunter—the grocery list of four men for two weeks need not cost more than $24. The only trouble in making up such a list is to know how to place our money to the best advantage, or, what quantities of different articles to buy. As a criterion of what is required,

I give below a list of groceries which were taken by three young hunters on an actual trip, and which gave perfect satisfaction and left no great surplus to be carried home. It is to be noted that this was a duck shooting excursion, by water, in birch bark canoes:

COMPARATIVE LIST OF PROVISIONS.
Three Men for Two Weeks:

Smoked ham	20 lbs
Pork (very fat)	20 lbs
Lard (for frying)	5 lbs
Corn Beef	3 cans
Lobster	4 cans
Salmon	4 cans
Boston Baked Beans	3 cans
Smoked Herrings	1 box
White Beans	8 pints
Flour	10 lbs
Oatmeal	10 lbs
Tea	2 lbs
Coffee	1 lb
Cocoa	2 pkgs
Pilot Bread	15 lbs
Brown Sugar	10 lbs
Rice	7 lbs

Cooking Raisins	2 lbs
Syrup	1 gal
Pickles	4 bottles
Marmalade	2 jars
Harvey's Sauce	2 bottles
Baking Powder	1 tin
Mixed Herbs	1 tin
Onions	10 lbs
Potatoes, and in same bag, a few carrots	1-2 bush
Salt, Pepper, Mustard, Vinegar.	

Bread, Butter, Eggs, Milk and Potatoes were purchased occasionally *en route*.

The above is a very simple list of plain food, but when to this is added the game secured, ducks, snipe and fish, we have the materials wherewith to concoct very elaborate meals. While this party were careful to go out fully provisioned for the two weeks of their intended stay, the game which they bagged enabled them to prolong their trip to three weeks, and thus they had the full pleasure of hunting without any fear of being stinted in their rations.

When going in pursuit of different game, through different descriptions of country, the kind of provisions which the hunter should carry varies somewhat, and it is therefore impossible to give any definite list by which he may be guided; but I think that reference to the list presented above, and a consideration of the methods advanced for ascertaining the quantity required, with a glance at the list in Section II, will enable him to arrive at a close estimate of what he actually requires, and to see what articles of luxury are at his disposal. To the amateur I can merely reiterate my admonition that he trust not to fickle chances of the chase, nor yet to the procurability of provisions *en route.*

SECTION II.

LIST OF PROVISIONS FROM WHICH TO SELECT.

That the hunter may see at a glance what articles are available, and that he may overlook none of the necessaries, I submit a list of such provisions as are suitable for his larder. When we take into consideration the varieties of canned goods which modern trade places at the disposal of the housekeeper, we have a very long list from which to select our provisions for camping out. But I wish to warn the young hunter against purchasing largely of canned goods. He will find them in most cases, to be very expensive food, and such as is apt to pall on the appetite. He will occasionally long for an honest dish of Ham and Eggs, Pork and Beans, Fried

Potatoes or Flap-jacks. Such canned goods as will be found most useful are as follows:

Cooked Corn Beef, Ham, Lobsters, Salmon, Baked Beans, Pea flour, Liebig's Extract of Beef, Lambs' Tongues, Sardines, Marmalade, Condensed Milk. We have in these the materials for cold lunches.

The long list of canned luxuries offered by most grocers is also open to inspection, and comprises

Canned **Soups,** in Tomato, Pea, Chicken, Oxtail, Maccaroni, Soup Bouilli, etc., Canned Oysters, Mackerel, **Deviled Ham,** Deviled **Meats,** Roast Lamb and **Mutton,** Smoked **Beef,** Tenderloin, Bonne **Bonche,** Pigs' Feet, **Corn,** Peas, **Succotash,** Tomatoes, Strawberries, Quinces, **Pears,** Peaches, **Pine Apples,** etc., and in sauces we have Harvey, **Nabob,** Browning, **Worcestershire,** Chutney, Tobasco, **French** and German **Mustard,** etc., and a host of other articles.

It may be observed that by taking a few cans of the luxuries the amateur **may** make his meals in the wilderness more like those at home, and so escape the unpleasant craving for food to which he has been used. I well remember that in our first trips into the wilds, when we carried no canned articles, our chief craving was for fresh meat, and when we failed to secure any game, and were forced to live on ham or salt pork day after day, this craving became very marked and detracted in no small degree from the pleasure of the trip. With our modern supply of canned meats, no hunter need experience this want.

The other groceries from which to select are, Ham, Pork, Lard, for frying, Codfish, Smoked Herrings, Flour, Oatmeal, Cornmeal, Potatoes, Onions, Carrots, Compressed Vegetables, White Beans, Cheese, Rice, Raisins, Brown Sugar, White Sugar, Syrup, Tea, Coffee, Cocoa, Chocolate, Broma, Kaoka, Pickles, Curry Powder, Baking Powder, Mixed Herbs, Corn Starch, Pilot Bread, and in fact the whole range of groceries, as necessity or fancy dictates. Do not forget those necessary articles, Salt, Pepper, Mustard, and Vinegar. Butter may be taken and also eggs, packed in salt, if these articles cannot be bought *en route*. Bread is too bulky to carry, and if we take plenty of flour we may bake our own.

SECTION III.

THE HUNTER'S PARAPHERNALIA.

When contemplating a trip, the hunter, especially if he be an amateur, should make out a list of every article which he will require, both in groceries and in personal belongings, and as each article is packed away in its proper place he should mark it off the list. In this way he will be sure to procure everything which may be needed, and he will escape the disagreeable experience of finding, when well on his journey, that some little but much needed article, such as salt, has been left behind.

The following list comprises the articles generally required when on a hunting trip *via* water:

If bark canoes are used, we should take a spare paddle, a pole, leg-of-mutton sail, canvas and tacks for repairs, a sponge, some rosin and a rosin pot and iron. This iron, being heated, is used to melt the old rosin on the canoe, and so cover leaks when they occur at seams which have been previously rosined. We may next enumerate the tent, with its bag, poles, ropes and pegs complete. A good long rope should be carried to secure the tent in gales, and will be found otherwise useful. Cooking utensils, per Section VII. Provisions, per Sections I and II.

Groceries may be best carried in strong cotton bags, holding each about 10 pounds, marked in pencil with the name of contents, and packed in water-proof boxes. These boxes should be the size of common biscuit boxes, for if they are too big and very heavy, when packed, they are awkward to handle.

Canned goods, potatoes, etc., which will not be injured by water, may be carried in bags, such as salt sacks. A sharp axe and a supply of matches are required. Matches may be carried in a large-mouthed bottle, securely corked, in a waterproof tin box.

We may enumerate other articles as follows: Gun, powder, shot, (different sizes) wads and caps, or cartridges for breech-loaders, cleaning utensils, rags and oil. Belt and hunting knife. A sewing bag containing needles, thread, etc., fishing outfit, wax candles, change of shirt, pants and socks for night. Mocassins for night, a tin of boot-grease, (see Section XI) blankets, water-proof bags to hold bedding and clothes, overcoat, Rubber coat, Cups, plates, knife, fork and spoon. Cloth for washing dishes. Each member should have a haversack containing towels, comb, brush, soap, tooth brush, handkerchief, etc. Such articles as tobacco may also be carried in the haversack. Reading matter may be carried if desired. Rubber sheets are excellent articles for spreading on the ground under the bedding, and for covering goods in rainy weather. Lastly, any medicines which may be thought requisite should be carried. (See section X.)

The experienced hunter will know without any remarks on my part, what of the above mentioned articles will be most useful to him, but to the amateur I would say that, so far as is commensurate with his capabilities of transportation, he is at liberty to consult his comfort, and should take with him on his trip, all articles which may actually conduct to his enjoyment of his holiday. He should be careful that all articles of his paraphernalia are properly packed in appropriate receptacles, so that in unloading his boat or canoe he will not have a multitude of loose articles to handle.

It is impossible to place before the amateur any absolute list of his requirements, but from the above table he will be able to select whatever he may need for any description of Hunting excursion.

SECTION IV.

THE CAMP FIRE.

The quality of our fire depends, of course, upon the wood which we find at hand, and somewhat, though not necessarily in any great degree, upon the state of the weather. In some localities wood is very scarce and we have to exercise great economy in its use. In such cases the fire should be built in a hole or trench so as to prevent drafts of air from hastening combustion. In selecting a permanent camping place, wood is one of the most important considerations. In some places quantities of drift wood abound, and when near by we have the standing hard wood, we are in the cook's paradise.

Care should be taken that the fire is not built too close to the tent, and also that it be placed to leeward thereof to prevent danger from sparks. In making our fire we first procure a large log, green if possible, and place it, lengthwise to the wind, on the spot chosen as our fire-place. This is called the "Back log," and against it we build our fire, on whichever side is most convenient. Over the Back log, from behind, project our cranes, or "spumgullions"—poles driven into the ground and notched on the upper side to receive the handles of our kettles, as they swing over the blaze. In laying the sticks for the fire we should place them all one way, parallel to the back log, and start the flame at the windward end. By laying the wood in this manner, we secure a more compact fire than when we cross-pile the sticks, and the sticks fall down to their own burning as those below are consumed; but if we cross-pile the sticks they fall apart when burnt through the middle, and necessitate a continual raking to keep them together. The object of placing the back log parallel to the wind is to prevent its being burned through the middle, and to allow us to work with greater ease on either side of the fire.

In undertaking the different methods of cooking, we require different kinds of fires. Thus, for boiling an ordinary fire will suffice, but for frying we require a good bed of coals and no blaze. This subject is more fully referred to in "General Remarks on Cooking," Section VII.

Before cooking each meal we should brush the loose ashes away from the fire with a bough. If we camp on the same spot for a few days, the accumulation of ashes at our fire place will be very inconvenient; and they should be covered with a thin layer of earth and the fire continued thereon, or we may select a new spot for the fire, covering the old ashes as before to prevent their being blown about. Should we wish to cook a very elaborate dinner, we should start two fires, about five yards apart, and so escape the great heat which one large fire would throw out. At one of these fires we may perform the roasting or frying; at the other, the boiling.

In rainy weather, when not being used for cooking, the fire should be covered with slabs of wood to shed the rain, or a frame work of poles should be erected over it and a rubber sheet, or a roof of bushes, placed thereon. If the fire is not kept burning all night some dry sticks should be placed under cover of the tent and will save much trouble in starting the fire in the morning when everything will be wet with dew.

Should the hunter be reduced to the necessity of using grass or hay with which to cook, he should twist the hay into tight ropes or blocks about two feet long and of three or four inches diameter. The tighter these blocks are compressed the longer they will burn, and the hotter will be the fire. It is a fact that on the Western Prairies, where wood is often extremely scarce, some farmers use this description of fuel for both the purposes of cooking and heating their habitations.

In using his axe to cut up fire wood, the amateur cannot employ too much care both to prevent accidents to himself or companions, and to avoid breaking the handle or dulling the axe on stones. For the production of fire a good supply of matches should be carried and the utmost care bestowed upon their safe keeping. The hunter will do well to provide himself with a sun, or burning glass, and if by any accident his matches are lost, this glass on being held at the proper focal distance, in the sunshine, will readily ignite paper, leaves, or small splints. But as this glass is available only during sunshine, it is well to have other methods of procuring fire at our command. If some paper or cloth be placed in a gun on a charge of powder, it will be ignited when the gun is fired, and may be coaxed into flame. Another method is to scatter some powder on a stone, and having placed some dry leaves on the powder in such a manner as to prevent these being blown away, explode a cap on the powder by a blow of the axe or a stone. The sparks produced by striking two stones together will also explode powder. In using these methods some of the powder should be dampened and formed into a ball. This will burn slowly and throw off a vast quantity of sparks, and produce great heat. Some of the uncivilized tribes of Polynesia procure fire by inserting a pointed stick into a corresponding hole in another piece of wood, and twirling the stick rapidly between the palms of the hands. This method may be looked upon as being the hunter's last resource, and I hope none of my readers will ever have to test its efficacy.

SECTION V.

GENERAL REMARKS ON CAMP ROUTINE.

For the guidance of the amateur who is not conversant with the General Economy of Camp life, I may present a series of short remarks on the system of management which he should follow when on an excursion. As the circumstances under which hunting trips are undertaken vary so widely, some being by land and in pursuit of different kinds of game, and some by water in various conveyances, it may be well if I confine myself to speaking of some definite kind of trip, and from the observations advanced the amateur may determine what method of management to pursue when on any kind of excursion. For the present, we may consider that the following remarks apply, in chief, to the conducting of a Duck shooting excursion, by water, in bark canoes.

The daily work in Camp, such as cooking, collecting wood, etc., should either be undertaken by each member in turn, or each member should be assigned a special duty for the whole trip.

If possible, go into Camp before dark, and have all arrangements completed before nightfall.

In selecting a Camping ground, the conditions to be desired are, plenty of wood, good water, with a convenient landing place, and a dry, level, sheltered spot for the tent.

A bed of spruce boughs may be made as follows: Cut off all large butts; lay the boughs in tiers, commencing at the top of the bed, placing the butts toward the bottom, and over this spread a rubber sheet or a blanket.

The blankets used at night should not be spread down in the daytime.

In case of rain, dig a small trench round the tent to prevent water from running in.

At night loosen the tent-ropes, as the dew causes the canvass to contract.

Guns may be strapped round the tent-poles; ammunition boxes placed at the head of the beds; grocery boxes, at night, placed inside the tent, ranged at the foot of the beds; haversacks suspended from the tent-poles, or kept at the head of the beds, or, in daytime, hung outside the tent.

Stretch a rope, high up between the tent-poles, on which to hang clothing at night. In daytime, the rope may be suspended outside for the same purpose, or a pole will answer the same end.

On rising in the morning spread all the bedding on the grass, if dry, to air; when taken in, fold it up neatly, and place each man's bundle at the head of his bed.

If, during a continuance of rainy weather, the bedding becomes damp, seize every opportunity of drying it before the fire.

When on an excursion for any length of time, such articles of clothing as shirts, socks, etc., may be washed on a fine day, and hung in the sun to dry.

At night, the canoes should be lifted out of the water, and may be placed on their sides close to the curtains of the tent as an additional shelter from the wind.

On breaking up Camp, or starting on a day's journey, examine and repair the canoes before loading up.

The consistency of which to make rosin depends on the season of the year and the temperature of the water. If too hard, the rosin splits or cracks in cold water, and if too soft it runs in warm weather. Use more or less grease according to circumstances. Wet the finger before applying it to press or smooth the rosin on the canoe.

When not in use, keep the canoe in the shade. Let it remain on its bottom in the grass if no shade is available.

When at the ponds for the evening shooting, the canoe should be hid in the bushes, or it may be masked by placing boughs and grass in it so as to hide the entire structure. When the canoe is thus disguised the hunter may sit in it to shoot, or he may paddle to within gun-shot of ducks in the water.

Cooking utensils, after being cleaned, and when not in use, should be ranged on a slab, or other piece of wood, near the fire-place. A small rack may also be erected here on which to hang dish-towels, etc.

Small saplings, stripped of their branches, but having the forks left on, may be driven into the ground on either side of the tent door, and will form excellent racks on which to hang shot-bags, belts, etc., during the day, and against which to lean paddles, fishing-poles, etc.

The grocery boxes should be over-hauled and cleaned occasionally, and all parcels examined and kept neatly tied up.

Place such groceries as are most used in a box by themselves.

Each member of the party should be acquainted with the whereabouts of every article.

This will prevent much mauling and tossing of goods. The maxim, "Have a place for everything, and keep everything in its place," should never be more strictly obeyed, and its observance is never followed by better results, than when in Camp.

Keep all dishes, knives. etc., in a box by themselves.

All articles which will admit of it should be carried in bags as these adapt themselves to any shape in the canoe, and contract as their contents diminish.

Ham and Pork should be wrapped in a clean, strong cloth, and may be carried in a bag.

Occasionally, on a fine day, the contents of all bags should be spread out in the sun, (that is, vegetables, and such articles as will be benefited thereby) and the bags allowed to get aired and dried.

Do not forget that the guns, being much used, require to be cleaned occasionally. Neat's-foot oil is excellent to use on locks, etc.

A rule which all amateurs should follow is, "Do not argue before breakfast."

Those who do not bathe for pleasure daily, when the opportunity presents, should make it a duty to do so.

Never fire at small birds with Duck-shot; it will be a waste of ammunition. Use the proper sizes of shot for different game.

If possible, let the Tent be dry before folding it up to remove.

When leaving a camping ground, and after the canoes are loaded, take a last look and examine the ground carefully, that nothing may be left behind.

When in the Canoe, the guns, if loaded, should occupy the following positions: The bow-man should rest his, hammers downward, on the bar in front of him, with the but running back by his knees; the stern-man also rests his against the bar in front of him, and in the same position as described for the bow, keeping the muzzle pointed outwards clear of the man in the bow. When in pursuit of game, or when passing through places where ducks may lurk, the bow-man should keep his gun in hand ready for action. Keep the gun, when loaded, except when required for immediate use, at half-cock, and in raising it in the Canoe elevate the muzzle first, and do not let the hammer catch on the bars, etc.

At all times, when carrying or holding a loaded gun, keep its muzzle elevated, or depressed, and pointing out of range of all persons.

Let the weight of each man be known, and in loading the Canoe distribute the cargo so that when manned she will float on an even keel.

When one person alone is paddling an empty Canoe, he will find it to be a great assistance to place a few stones in the bow as ballast, especially if the wind be blowing.

For sailing in a Canoe a *leg-of-mutton* sail is generally used. The mast is strapped into a notch in the back edge of the fore-mid bar, and its heel fits into a small step screwed to the ribs beneath.

Two Canoes may be lashed together and blankets or sheets used as sails. The Canoes are placed at about four feet apart at the center bars, and the tent-poles, are securely lashed across to the fore-mid and aft-mid bars of each Canoe. The lashings should be securely fastened at each gunnel at each bar. The sail may be placed in either Canoe, or each may carry one. When sailing in this manner before the wind, great speed may be attained with perfect safety.

When passing over good bottoms, the pole may be used as a pleasant change from paddling, but none but those who are well practiced in the art should venture to pole a loaded Canoe.

In going down stream, keep the current; in going up, hug the shore.

. If the hunter has to pass through dangerous rapids, he should lash all his valuable articles to the canoe and divest himself of shoes and all superflous clothing.

From the foregoing remarks, the amateur will gather that all is required to render his life in Camp pleasant, and to crown with success his efforts at house-keeping in the wilderness, is some small stock of neatness and activity, and in fact that he follow, in some degree, the well-recognized customs of civilized households.

SECTION VI.

COOKING UTENSILS.

Regular Trappers can and often do perform their cooking with a surprisingly small number of utensils. In fact, a kettle for tea is the stock in trade of many. Their game is spitted before the glowing coals or roasted in a bed of ashes in the midst of the fire, and potatoes or bread are baked before the open fire. Thus they rival in the limited resources of their *cuisine*, the paucity of those Kings of the Chase, the red denizens of the primeval prairies. And yet those old trappers are perfectly happy, and for the best of reasons, that they have never known any other mode of living. I do not mean to say that they are ignorant of the customs of civilization, I merely state that they are so accustomed to their mode of living that they do not desire, and would not be content, under any other circumstances. But I do not expect the amateur hunter to confine himself to such a limited list of cooking utensils. The man who devotes but a few days in a year to the exciting chase may be allowed, in following out the same line of conduct as that pursued by the professional hunter, to retain, as far as he wishes, the habits of his daily life. He should not feel called upon to stint himself of any comforts when selecting his cooking utensils for a trip.

For excursions to different localities, by different modes of conveyance, and for different periods of time, the number and description of cooking utensils required varies greatly. Nevertheless, I present a full list of these articles, and the hunter can easily decide what he will require, both as necessities or as attributes to his greater comfort.

The first and most important article of our

list of cooking utensils, is the tea kettle—most important, for only in one way can we prepare this cheering beverage. This may be of tin, and should be of a capacity suitable to the number composing the hunting party. One kettle, if kept properly clean, will very well answer for the making up both tea and coffee.

Next we have the Frying-pan. This is an old stand-by for hunters, and a most useful article. All kinds of fish, flesh and fowls may be cooked in this ever-ready utensil. There is a pan made expressly for cooking at the camp fire, having a long iron handle, but this instrument I cannot recommend. The handle is heavy and unwieldy. For our greater comfort in cooking we may attach a long wooden handle to the short iron one of the pan, tying it thereto with twine or wire. This handle may be detached, if so desired, for greater ease of transportation. If necessary, two frying pans may be carried, and while one is employed in frying fish or ham, the other may be used for frying potatoes, warming beans, etc., or for stewing articles. The second pan will well repay the trouble of transportation.

We next want the utensils in which to cook our potatoes, beans, rice or oatmeal. For potatoes, a tin kettle will suffice, but if possible, an iron pot should be carried for cooking the other articles as they burn very easily when cooked in tin. Nevertheless, a tin kettle will do very well, requiring but a little more attention to keep the contents well stirred and the fire in a moderate condition. It is a good plan to have kettles of different sizes, such as will fit inside one another. In this way we greatly increase our abilities to cook without sacrificing space in transportation.

A Dutch Oven is an excellent article on a hunting excursion, and should be taken when space in the boat or canoe will permit. Its use is referred to in Section VII.

There are a variety of cooking appliances manufactured for the use of the hunter, such as the "Tripod and Utensils" and "The Camp Cooking Stove" with its compactly arranged pots, but for cooking at the open camp fire the utensils mentioned above are all that are necessary. To enumerate, we may say that the cooking utensils required on an ordinary hunting trip—for example, a Duck shooting excursion, *via* water, in canoes, a party of four, for ten days—are as follows:

    1 Tea Kettle, tin.
    1 Potato Kettle, tin.
    1 Rice, etc., Kettle, iron preferred.
    1 or 2 Fry Pans.
    Dutch Oven, if possible.

When we remember that we can roast our game before the fire, or burried in the ashes, it will be seen that, with the above utensils, our methods of cooking are as uncurtailed as if we had a domestic cooking range on which to manipulate our meals

Great care should be taken of the cooking utensils, and to much attention cannot be paid to keeping them clean. Section VI contains some remarks further relating to the hunters' Cooking Utensils. and should be read in this connection.

SECTION VII.

GENERAL REMARKS ON CAMP COOKING.

When *en route*, and the chief object is to cover distance, the hunter has little time to bestow on cooking. He then falls back on his canned goods, and probably confines his efforts at cooking to the production of the ever-acceptable can of Tea. But when in a stationary camp, and, indeed, whenever he can spare time when *en route*, the hunter should put forth his best efforts and produce at least one solid, substantial and comfortable meal per day. To the person who is at all conversant with the art of cooking, the preparing of such a meal is an absolute pleasure. More especially does he feel gratified if his companions on the trip are deficient in knowledge of cooking, for, in truth, the experienced cook then becomes the most important personage in the party, and he also has the pleasure of knowing that his efforts are appreciated, for the good will of hunters, as well as that of the proverbial morose husband, is reached through their stomachs. Though such a person may be quite willing to undertake the cooking for his party, during the entire trip, yet a more desirable state of affairs exists when all the party are able to undertake that important duty in rotation. (We refer, of course, to parties who have no hired cook with them.) No party should ever venture to go out on a hunting excursion without numbering in their ranks at least one person who can cook. It appears to be foolish to write such an evident, simple remark, but when amateur hunters act foolishly, must I not suit my conversation to their comprehension? I have known parties to act just thus foolishly. I once met with a party of young men on an excursion, and far from home. They had a good supply of provisions with them, but, from sheer ignorance of how to cook their food, they were glad to buy meals at the houses of farmers on the way. But we will revert to a more pleasant part of our subject—we will endeavor, as is one of the chief objects of this pamphlet, to teach such young amateur hunters how to enjoy, to its fullest, their food.

In cooking, be it in the kitchen of kings, or at the humble camp fire of the hungry hunter, too much attention cannot be paid to that God-like quality—cleanliness. All our cooking utensils should undergo close inspection before being used, and after use they should be cleaned and put away in their proper place. All articles to be cooked should be thoroughly cleaned, and the cook himself would do well to pay a little attention to personal cleanliness before he undertakes to exercise his art. Look you! of what more disgusting object can we conceive than the person who, rousing from his blankets in camp, proceeds to prepare the morning meal with utensils which, though musty from last night's supper, are yet clean when compared with his unsanctified condition? The sight of a slovenly, dirty person cooking our food detracts in no small degree from our appetite. If several of the party are able to assist in preparing a meal, one should collect wood and attend to the fire; another may clean such articles as game, potatoes. etc., so that he who undertakes to superintend the cooking may give his undivided attention to the handling of the small groceries. If the cook has no assistance, he should so regulate his work that all the rougher tasks are completed first, so that he may wash his hands before undertaking the more delicate office of manipulating the ingredients of his various dishes. The cook must not forget that different articles vary in the length of time required to cook them, and he should place on the fire first those requiring the longest time; he will thus have all his articles ready for table at once, and nothing need be allowed to get cold.

ON BOILING.

This is the simplest method of preparing food, and by it almost every description of fish, meat, fowls and vegetables may be cooked. When in camp we need not confine the operation of boiling to any particular description of kettle; we may even boil articles in our frying pan, the essential condition of the operation being merely that the articles are cooked in boiling water. It is to be noted that soups, stews, etc., are made by boiling, and owe their names to their ingredients rather than to the utensils in which they are prepared. The hunter may often be called upon to use the utensils at his command for purposes far different from those for which, in the economy of civilization, they were intended.

In boiling articles the hunter must pay attention to the following points :—the pot must be kept boiling, and not allowed to cease boiling until the article is cooked; boil slowly; know the time required to cook the article (given in the different recipes) and abide by it; skim the pot when a scum is seen to form on the surface. When the object is to extract substance from scraps of meat, or from bones, as in making soups, the pot may be allowed to boil faster, but should be kept closely covered. The following remark, taken from an excellent authority on Cooking, may be of interest, as it will apply as well to any articles which the hunter may cook, as to the meat spoken of. "Two mutton chops were covered with cold water, and one boiled fiercely, and the other simmered gently, for three-quarters of an hour; the flavor of the chop which was simmered was decidedly superior to that of the one which was boiled; the liquor which boiled fast was in like proportion more savoury, and, when cold, had much more fat on its surface; this explains why quick boiling renders meat hard, etc.,—because its juices are extracted in a greater degree." When the water evaporates quickly, more hot water should be added. Some remarks on the boiling of Vegetables will be found under that head in the recipes.

ON ROASTING AND BAKING.

A method of roasting fish and game, much in vogue with old hunter's, is to cover them up in a bed of hot coals, where they remain until cooked. This method is not to be recommended to amateurs. Nevertheless, he will find, in the recipes, directions for its use, and he may experiment with some fish or game on which he does not depend for a meal. Great experience is required to ensure its successful accomplishment. A simpler method of roasting is by spitting his game before a good clear fire. It is thus continually under his surveillance, and the operation should be as successful as it is simple. A pan should be placed under the article being roasted to catch the fat which exudes. A little water should be placed in the pan, with some salt, and the article cooking should be frequently basted with this liquor. The fire should not be too hot at first, as, by hardening the outside of the meat, it prevents the heat from penetrating. When about half cooked, the meat may be placed nearer the fire, or the fire increased. The time required to roast various articles is given in the recipes. The Spit is merely a stick inserted in the meat or game to be roasted, and serves to hold the article before the fire. It may be laid over a forked stick, or supported in any manner found convenient. The article being roasted should be frequently turned, and basted as before stated.

Baking, in our domestic kitchens, consists of placing the article to be cooked in the oven, and observing various regulations. Such an operation we, of course never perform when on a hunting excursion, but we can bake bread, potatoes, etc., before the fire in the same manner as we roast meat. There is no difference in the operations; the articles operated upon bestow the name on the method of operation. Thus our bread is *baked*, our game *roasted*.

Bread, and all compound dishes may be best baked in a Dutch Oven, and the amateur who considers his comfort should, when possible, have one of these articles among his cooking utensils. The oven his placed before a hot bed of coals, and by collecting the heat, and by reflection, readily cooks any articles consigned to its care.

ON FRYING.

Frying may be termed the hunter's rough and ready method of preparing food. By this method all fishes, flesh, and fowls may be cooked. The following points should be observed:—Have a clear fire of coals; make the pan hot and grease it well before placing articles in it to cook; olive oil is better than lard or other grease; if using pork fat, cut it up and try out, and place the meat in the remaining oil; all articles should be frequently turned to allow the steam to evaporate; shake the pan often, and do not allow the articles to stick; take care that the sputtering fat does not take fire, and if it does, remove the pan at once from the coals and blow out the blaze. The observing of these points, and of the directions found in the different recipes, should enable the hunter to attain complete success in frying his pan-cakes, ham and eggs, trout or birds.

ON STEWING.

The term Stewing is applied to the production of compound dishes, in which the various ingredients are boiled together. By this method we can produce many savoury and fragrant dishes. Stewing is also an economical process, for we may thus cook together scraps of meat, small birds and other articles which alone would prove to be but sorry morsels. It has been stated that all cookery is but an aid to digestion, and while I hold that some cookery may be very detrimental to the digestive organs, I will acknowledge that the process of stewing resembles the action of the stomach, and is therefore, if from no other reason, to be highly recommended to the hunter's use. The points to be observed when stewing articles are as follows:—let the pot boil slowly; stir frequently to prevent burning, and keep the pot continually boiling until the mass is cooked. Further remarks on stewing will be found in all recipes for preparing dishes by that useful method.

The hunter who carries the requisite utensils has all of the methods of cooking just mentioned at his command, and he must be indeed shiftless who, being provided with a sufficiency of good food, can not prepare it in such a manner that he may not only eat it, but also enjoy it to its fullest extent. In closing this Section, I may quote the following from an excellent authority:—"To some extent the claims of either process of cooking depend upon the taste of the individual. Some persons may esteem the flavor of fried meats, while others will prefer broils or stews. It is important, however, to understand the theory of each method of cooking, so that whichever may be adopted, it may be done well. Bad cooking, though by a good method is far inferior to good cooking by a bad method."

INDEX TO RECEIPTS.

RECEIPTS FOR CAMP COOKERY, (SEC. VIII.)

No.   Page.

SOUPS.

	General Remarks	61
1	Plain Pea Soup	63
2	Bean Soup	64
3	Liebig's Extract of Beef.	64
4	Canned Soups	65
5	Vegetable Soups	65

FISH.

6	Smoked Herrings	66
7	Fish, to bake in the coals	67
8	Fish, ordinary method of cooking	68
9	Brook Trout	68
10	Salmon	68
	Codfish. (See No. 89.)	108
	Fish-cakes. (See Nos. 90-91.)	109-110

CANNED FISH.

11	Oysters, stewed	69
12	Oysters, fried	70
13	Oysters, raw	70
14	Lobsters, as canned	70
15	Lobsters, stewed	70
16	Lobster Salad	71
17	Lobster Croquettes	71
18	Salmon, as canned	71
19	Salmon, stewed	72

GAME.

20	Venison, moose, bear-meat, etc., to roast	72
21	Ducks, partridges, quails, etc., roasting in the ashes	73
22	Ducks, partridges, squirrels, etc., roasting before the fire	73
23	Ducks, to stew	74
24	Ducks, to fry	75
25	Snipes, to fry	76
26	Snipes, to stew	76
27	Snipes, on toast	77
28	Turkey, to boil	77
29	Goose, to roast	78
30	Rabbit, to roast	78
31	Rabbit, curried	79
32	Rabbit, with onions	79

MISCELLANEOUS MEATS.

33	Salt Beef and Pork, stewed	80
34	Corned Beef, canned, cold	80
35	Corned Beef, canned, stewed	81
36	Ham, Bacon or Pork, to fry	81
37	Ham, Bacon or Pork, to roast or bake	82
38	Ham and Eggs	82
39	Ham or Pork, with onions	83
40	Ham, barbecued	84
41	Pork fritters	84
42	Pork and Beans. No. 1	85
43	Pork and Beans. No. 2	85
44	Eggs, to poach	86
45	Eggs, to boil	86
46	Eggs, Savory	87
47	Eggs, curried	87

INDEX TO RECEIPTS.

VEGETABLES.

48	Potatoes, to bake	88
49	Potatoes, to boil	88
50	Potatoes, (raw) fried	89
51	Potatoes, (boiled) fried	89
52	Potato fritters	89
53	Onions, to boil	90
54	Onions, to fry	90
55	Vegetables, miscellaneous . . .	91
56	Vegetables, canned	91

MISCELLANEOUS DISHES.

57	Rice, plain boiled	92
58	Rice, with raisins	92
59	Rice, savory	92
60	Rice croquettes	93
61	Rice pudding	93
62	Oatmeal pancakes	93
63	Flour pancakes	94
64	Indian Meal pancakes	95
65	Oatmeal porridge	95
66	Corn Meal porridge	96
67	Corn Meal porridge, fried . . .	96
68	Hoe Cake	96
69	Corn Bread	97
70	Oat Cake	97
71	Bread	98

PUDDINGS.

72	Batter pudding, baked or boiled . .	98
73	Rice pudding	99
74	Cossacks' Plum pudding . . .	99

SALAD-DRESSINGS AND SAUCES.

75 Dressing for Canned Lobster, etc. . . . 100
76 Tomato Salad 101
77 Dutch sauce, for Meat or Fish . . . 101
78 Sauce for Ducks, Geese, etc. 101
79 Drawn Butter, for Fish, Onions, etc. . . 102
80 Pudding sauce 102
81 Sauce Hollandaise, or Drawn Butter . . 103
82 Plum pudding Sauce 103

BEVERAGES.
Tea, General Remarks.

83 Tea, to steep or draw 105
84 Coffee, to draw 106
85 Coffee, to improve flavor of 107
86 Coffee, substitute for cream in . . . 107
87 Coffee, Essence or Extract of . . . 107
88 Beverages, miscellaneous 108

APPENDIX.

89 Codfish, salt, to boil 108
90 Fish Cakes, with raw fish 109
91 Fish Cakes, with cooked fish 110

THE LAST RESOURCE, OR WHAT TO USE WHEN PROVISIONS RUN SHORT. (Sec. IX.)
General Remarks.

92 Potato soup 113
93 Dandelions, as greens 114
94 Corn Meal 114
95 Frogs, to roast, fry or stew 115
96 Miscellaneous articles of diet . . . 115

SECTION VIII.

RECEIPTS FOR CAMP COOKERY.

NOTE.—If the hunter should wish to prepare any of the compound dishes mentioned in these Receipts, he must remember to include the different ingredients in his list of groceries. In all the receipts the quantities may be varied, but the proportions should be observed.

SOUP.

GENERAL REMARKS.

Soups are seldom made at the Camp fire, but as times may occur when scraps of meat and carcasses of game might be concocted into a fragrant dish, I feel that these Receipts would not be complete without some reference being made to Soups. As a general rule soups may be made out of any flesh or game which will impart its substance and flavor to the water. Canned soups are excellent articles of diet, and when we have a jar of Liebig's Extract of Beef we can produce a soup unrivalled in the whole range of cookery for its wholesome and sustaining qualities. Soups should be allowed to boil for a long time in order that the full substance of the article operated upon may be extracted. The soup should boil slowly and be frequently skimmed. In making soups in camp we wish to produce a good strong article, rather than the clear, delicate dish of society dinners. To this end it is a good plan to place a small quantity of vegetables, properly cut up, in the pot when first placing it on the fire. In the time required to extract the substance from the meat these vegetables will have dissolved, and will be thoroughly incorporated with the liquor. Other vegetables may be added at such times as will allow of their being cooked without their dissolving. Thus, carrots may be put in three-quarters of an hour before the soup is to be taken off the fire; potatoes and onions, twenty minutes before. All vegetables for soups should be thoroughly cleaned, cut into small pieces, and placed in cold water ready to add to the soup when required. In thickening soups with flour, the flour should be mixed with cold water and all lumps broken up, and then stirred into the boiling soup. Should the hunter have to place himself on short rations, he will find the soup pot to be his best friend.

1.

PLAIN PEA SOUP.

Put 3 pounds pork, well soaked, and cut into 4 or 5 pieces, into 3 quarts water. Add 1-2 pound split peas, 1-2 teaspoonful sugar, a little pepper, 3 ounces fresh vegetables or 2 ounces compressed. Boil 2 hours, or until peas are tender. Broken biscuit may be added. Salt beef may be used instead of pork, but should be well soaked. Do not add vegetables until the meat and peas have boiled an hour and a half.

2.

BEAN SOUP.

To 1 gallon water add 1 1-2 pints white beans, 2 pounds pork, or a ham bone, 4 onions cut fine, and pepper. Boil until beans are dissolved. If the beans have been soaked in water for some time, say over night, about 2 hours will suffice to cook them.

3.

LIEBIG'S EXTRACT OF BEEF.

That the hunter may see the full value of this article, I quote the following from the wrapper accompanying the pots: "A quarter of a teaspoonful of Extract dissolved in boiling water will, with the addition of a sufficient quantity of salt, produce a breakfast cupful of strong and clear Beef tea." This is an excellent beverage to partake of in the early morning before undertaking to prepare the regular breakfast. "An excellent soup, equal to that prepared from fresh meat, is obtained by boiling soup vegetables, with some bones and marrow, till done, and then adding the necessary quantity of Extract, with plenty of salt. Soups made with peas, lentils, beans, potatoes, bread, barley, carrots, turnips, and other vegetables, gain by the addition of Extract as much as if fresh meat had been boiled with them, equal in quantity to what would be required for producing the Extract."

4.

The canned soups sold by grocers, are to be recommended. Directions for use accompany each can or package.

5.

VEGETABLE SOUP.

(A good dish to use when rations run short.)

3 onions, 3 small turnips, 1 carrot, and 4 potatoes, all cut up. Put into the pot with

1-4 pound butter, same of lean ham, or any bones or scraps of meat, and a pinch of mixed herbs. Place over fire for 10 minutes, then add a spoonful of flour well mixed in 2 quarts of water, and a dessertspoonful Extract of Beef, (if on hand,) salt and pepper. Boil until vegetables are well cooked, skim, and serve with toasted bread.

FISH.

(Under this head we have the canned fish which we may purchase for our larder, as well as those which we may catch with the fly, or hook and line).

6.

SMOKED HERRINGS.

The simplest way to cook these fish is to toast them, at the end of a pointed stick over the coals, first cleaning and removing the skin. Another method is to scald in boiling water until the skin curls up, then remove head, tail and skin. Clean well. Put into fry pan with a little butter or lard. Fry gently a few minutes, dropping in a little vinegar. These are excellent articles on a trip, and may, if occasion arises, be eaten without any more cooking than what they received in being smoked.

7.

BAKING FISH IN THE COALS.

Clean the fish, and if it is large enough to be emptied through a hole in the neck, do not slit the belly. Season the inside with salt and pepper, and if liked, stuff with Indian meal. Have ready a good bed of glowing coals, and lay the fish in this and cover it up, using first some ashes or dead embers, that the fish may not be burnt. Half an hour, more or less, according to size, is required for the operation. Experience alone can determine the time required. On removing the fish from the fire and peeling off the skin, the flesh will be found to be clean and well soaked. The amateur should experiment in this method before he undertakes to trust to it for the production of a meal.

8.

ORDINARY METHOD OF COOKING FISH.

All fish, eels included, may be cooked by frying, the larger ones being cut up into several pieces. After cleaning the fish, wipe and dry well in a cloth. Place in the hot pan with plenty of fat. Sprinkle with indian meal. Turn frequently and shake the pan often. Season with salt, pepper, and a few drops of any sauce desired.

9.

BROOK TROUT.

If small, fry as directed in No. 8. If large, boil and serve with drawn butter. (No. 79.)

10.

SALMON.

Salmon may be boiled and served with drawn butter (No. 79) or cut into pieces and fried. Time of boiling varies according to size. Add salt to the water in which it is boiled.

CANNED FISH.

Directions for use are generally printed on the cans. The following will be found useful:

11.

OYSTERS, STEWED.

Pour the liquor off the oysters into the fry pan to stew with twice the quantity of milk. Add a little butter, the size of a marble, some salt and pepper, and a little crumbled biscuit, or thicken with a little flour. As soon as the liquor boils throw in the oysters and let them remain for 30 seconds. Then pour into dish for immediate use. When milk cannot be had, use water, same quantity as the liquor of the oysters, and to the above named ingredients add a pinch of mixed herbs. A few drops of lemon juice is an improvement, when herbs are not used.

12.

OYSTERS, FRIED.

Dry the oysters in a clean cloth. Dip in beaten egg and then in biscuit crumbs. Or sprinkled with Indian meal. Add salt and pepper. Fry for four or five minutes in lard, which is better for this purpose than butter. Turn them when necessary.

13.

OYSTERS, RAW.

When oysters are used raw, as canned, add salt, pepper and vinegar to suit the taste.

14.

LOBSTER, AS CANNED.

When lobsters are eaten cold, as prepared in the cans, the salad given in No. 75, will be an excellent addition.

15.

LOBSTER STEW.

Chop the lobster fine, add a little milk or water, 2 raw beaten eggs, and a small lump of butter. Stew in frying pan for five minutes. Salt and pepper to taste.

16.

LOBSTER SALAD.

Mix olive oil, mustard, vinegar, salt and a hard boiled egg. Beat up together, add lobster, lettuce and seasoning to suit the taste. Sliced cucumber or tomato may be substituted for lettuce.

17.

LOBSTER CROQUETTES.

Chop the lobster fine; add pepper and salt. Mix with one fourth as much bread crumbs as there is meat. Form into balls with 2 tablespoons of melted butter. Dip in beaten egg and roll in biscuit crumbs. Fry in lard.

18.

SALMON, AS CANNED.

Add salt, pepper and vinegar to suit taste.

19.

SALMON, STEWED.

Some people cannot eat canned salmon; they find that it poisons them. These unpleasant effects will not be experienced if the fish is prepared as follows:—Pour off all the oil and place the salmon in a little water in the fry pan. Let simmer for a minute, and pour off the water. Add a little fresh water, and thicken with flour, or bread or biscuit crumbs. Salt, pepper and a pinch of mixed herbs to suit the taste. Stew gently for five minutes.

GAME.

(All game should be kept for a day or two before being used, if the weather will permit.

20.

Venison, moose, or bear meat may be spitted in joints of several pounds before the fire, turning occasionally and sprinkling with salt and pepper. Baste as required. (See "General Remarks, Camp Cookery,"—Roasting.) Use any sauce preferred.

21.

Ducks, partridges, quail, etc., may be roasted in the coals in the manner described for fish in No. 7. Draw and clean in the usual manner, but do not pluck off the feathers. Stuff with bread crumbs or broken biscuit well seasoned with salt and pepper. Dip the bird in water to wet the feathers, and bury in the ashes and coals. The time required can only be judged by experience; the size of bird and strength of fire are to be considered. A teal will require half an hour or more, other birds proportionately. When taken from the fire remove the skin, and if the operation has been successful the flesh will be found to be clean and tender. (For sauces for game see No. 78.)

22.

Ducks, partridges, pigeons, turkeys, geese, black-birds, snipes, squirrels, etc., may be spitted before the fire. Clean the birds well, and observe the directions given for "Game" in No. 20. The birds may be split open down the back and extended on the spitting stick, or they may be roasted whole, with appropriate dressings. (For dressings see No. 78, etc.) Time required to roast Woodcock or Snipe, 15 or 20 minutes. Pheasant or Partridge, 20 or 30 minutes. Duck, 45 minutes, Turkey, 3 hours for a large one: 2 hours for middling size.

23.

DUCKS, ALL KINDS, TO STEW.

Clean well and divide into convenient pieces. Place in the pot in enough cold water to cover them, or as much as you will require to produce the desired quantity of stew. Place on the fire and boil slowly. Add salt, pepper, and a pinch of mixed herbs, Worcestershire or other sauce to suit taste, also some onions, carrots, potatoes, etc., cut fine. A few of these vegetables may be placed in the pot when first put to the fire. They will dissolve in the time required to stew the game, and add a pleasant *body* to the dish. Time required, about one hour and a half. The remainder of vegetables may be added as follows: carrots, about 45 minutes before stew will be cooked; potatoes, onions, or turnips, about 30 minutes. If vegetables are not used to thicken the stew, by being allowed to dissolve, a little flour or corn starch may be used for that purpose. To stew slowly for a long time is the secret of success in making these stews, and yet the pot must be removed from the fire as soon as the meat is sufficiently cooked. Inspect the meat occasionally and you will know just when it is done. Do not let the contents of the pot burn at the bottom. Skim the pot frequently.

24.

DUCKS, TO FRY.

Having cleaned and plucked the bird, divide into pieces, such as legs, wings, and make four pieces of the body. Dry the meat in a cloth, and place in the hot frying pan with some pork fat previously tried out. Season with salt, pepper, and any sauce desired. Fry slowly until done. Remove the meat from the pan and set in a dish by the fire to keep warm. Then to the fat in the pan add a little water (sufficient to make the desired quantity of sauce) thicken with flour, to which has been added an onion chopped fine and some mixed herbs. Stir briskly until incorporated, and stew for about five minutes. Pour over the fried duck, and serve.

25.

SNIPES, TO FRY.

Same as for Ducks, (No. 24) but do not cut the birds up after cleaning. Omit onion from the sauce.

26.

SNIPES, TO STEW.

Same method as for Ducks, (No. 23.) Place 6, 10, or 12 birds in the pot, whole, at once. If the birds are very fat, remove the fat before stewing them. Skim pot frequently.

27.

SNIPE ON TOAST.

After dressing the birds fasten a very thin piece of fat ham or bacon round the breast of each and fry in boiling hot lard for two minutes. Sprinkle with pepper and salt, and serve each on a piece of toast.

28.

TURKEY, TO BOIL.

Pluck the bird carefully, draw and singe it; wash it inside with warm water. Wipe dry with a cloth. Cut off the head and neck close to the backbone, leaving enough of the crop skin to turn over the stuffing. Draw the sinews from the legs, and cut off the feet just below the first joint of the leg. Press the legs into the sides and skewer them firmly. Fill the breast with sausage or forcemeat, or bread crumbs, herbs and onions. Put into sufficient hot water to cover it; boil gently for from one and a half to two hours. Remove the scum as it rises. (For sauces see Nos. 78, 79, 81.)

29.
GOOSE, TO ROAST.

Having picked, cleaned and singed the bird make a stuffing as follows: 2 ounces onion (if the flavor of raw onions is not liked, slice and partly boil them) chopped fine; 1 ounce sage or mixed herbs; 4 ounces bread crumbs, stale; a lump of butter, size of a walnut, and a little pepper and salt. Mix the whole well together with the yolks of two eggs. Do not quite fill the goose, as the stuffing will swell. Tie it to the spit at both ends, and roast for an hour and a half, or an hour and three quarters.

30.
RABBIT, TO ROAST.

Skin and clean thoroughly, and spit before a good fire. (Observe the directions given in "General Remarks on Cooking,"—Roasting.)

31.

RABBIT, CURRIED.

Skin and wash the rabbit and cut it into joints. Put on to stew with 2 ounces butter and 3 onions sliced. When the onions are brown pour in one pint of stock, made with Extract of Beef. (See No. 3.) The stock should be boiling when added to the stew. Mix 1 tablespoonful of curry powder and 1 tablespoonful flour smoothly with a little water and add to the stew. Stew slowly for half an hour or more. A little lemon juice is an improvement. Serve with boiled rice.

32.

RABBIT WITH ONIONS.

Clean the Rabbit and put it on to boil in enough cold water to cover it. When boiled tender take it out, joint it, and fry in lard to a light brown. Remove from the pan and set by the fire to keep warm. Have six onions sliced, and fry them in the lard.

When done add a little water and a tablespoonful of flour. Let this simmer for a minute, and pour over the rabbit.

MISCELLANEOUS MEATS.

33.

SALT BEEF AND PORK STEWED.

Cut the beef and pork, or either, into dice and place in the pot or pan to stew. If the meat is very salt the water may be poured off after stewing for 2 minutes, and fresh water added. After stewing gently for half an hour, add vegetables, carrots, potatoes, etc., and some pepper and mixed herbs. Thicken with flour or rice. When vegetables are cooked, remove the stew and add toasted bread, or broken biscuit.

34.

CANNED CORNED BEEF, COLD.

After removing the beef from the can, cut into slices, and use with pepper, mustard, and Worcestershire, or any other sauce to suit taste. Canned beef should be kept in a cool place, and placed in cold water for some time before being opened.

35.

CANNED CORNED BEEF, STEWED.

Stew together some carrots, onions and potatoes, or some compressed vegetables, with herbs, pepper and salt to taste, and when nearly cooked add as much canned beef as desired. Let simmer until the gelatine in the beef has become incorporated with the stew—between 5 and 10 minutes.

36.

HAM, BACON, OR PORK, TO FRY.

The simple operation of frying these meats is properly understood by few. The following points should be attended to:—The slices cut should not be more than one-eighth of an inch thick. If very salt, and these meats generally are, the slices should be soaked in warm water for at least an hour, and the water changed two or three times. If this does not extract the salt sufficiently, the slices may be boiled for a short time before frying. After soaking, pare off all rind, etc., and trim nicely. Wipe and dry the slices before placing in the pan. Have the pan hot and well greased, and fry the slices quickly until brown, turning them when necessary. Add pepper and sauce to taste.

37.

HAM, BACON OR PORK, TO ROAST OR BAKE.

The slices of ham, etc., as cut and prepared as dictated in No. 36, may be roasted before the fire on a spit, or rolled up and secured with a wooden skewer, and baked in the Dutch oven.

38.

HAM AND EGGS.

Prepare the ham as directed in No. 36. (For this purpose the slices may be cut a little thicker if so wished.) When fried remove from pan and set by the fire. See that the pan is not very hot, and break into it the desired number of eggs. In doing this hold the egg very near the pan, and do not let it spread much. The pan must be held very steady until the eggs are set. Dip a little of the hot grease over the eggs. Add pepper and salt if necessary. When the eggs are cooked place each on a slice of ham and serve. A nicer method of preparing eggs for this dish is by poaching them in water. (See No. 44.)

39.

HAM, OR PORK, AND ONIONS.

Prepare the ham, etc., as directed in No. 36, and place by the fire to keep warm. Have ready some onions, say 2 per man, previously sliced and stewed until nearly cooked, with pepper, some herbs if liked, and salt if necessary. On taking the ham from the pan, place the onions, from which drain the water, in it and fry for about 5 minutes. Add a tablespoonful moist flour. Turn over the ham or pork, and serve. (See No. 54.)

40.

BARBECUED HAM.

Prepare as in No. 36, then lay the slices in the pan, pepper each, and spread on each one-fourth teaspoon of made mustard. Pour in vinegar in proportion of half a teaspoonful to a slice; fry quickly, turning often. Remove and place on a dish. Then add to gravy half a glass of wine, if on hand, and one teaspoonful sugar, boil up once and pour over the slices of ham.

41.

PORK FRITTERS.

Prepare slices of pork as directed in No. 36. Place in pan and fry until nearly done. Have at hand a thick batter made of one part corn meal to two parts flour, mixed with cold water. Dip the slices of pork in the batter, and replace in fry pan until cooked a nice brown.

42.

PORK AND BEANS. NO. 1.

Soak 1 quart beans over night. Next day boil with 1 large onion. When nearly done take out the onion, and place the beans in a dish to bake before the fire, or in Dutch oven. In centre of beans put 1-2 pound salt pork, not fully buried. Pour in some of the water in which the beans were boiled, and bake one hour.

43.

PORK AND BEANS. NO. 2.

Boil the beans, (time about 3 hours) and when half done add pieces of pork, some pepper and an onion cut fine. If water evaporates, add more, but regulate so that when the beans are boiled there will be no water to pour off. Do not bake. A supply of these beans may be kept for some days in a jar, and warmed in a frying pan, etc., as required.

44.

EGGS, TO POACH.

Have some water, well salted, simmering in the frying pan, and into this break the eggs, one at a time, carefully, so as not to break the yolk. Let the egg run slowly from the shell, holding the hand as near the water as possible. Dip the hot water over the eggs. Remove them before they are hard. Time about two and a half minutes. Place each upon a piece of thin buttered toast. This is an excellent way of preparing eggs to eat with fried ham or pork. (See No. 38.)

45.

EGGS, TO BOIL.

Time required, to boil soft, three minutes. After that time they become hard. The water should not be boiling violently, as it is then liable to burst the shell and spoil the egg. Place the egg gently in the pot, as a very slight blow will crack the shell.

46.

SAVORY EGGS.

Break 5 eggs into a dish, add a pinch of salt, pepper and thyme, or mixed herbs; beat them well together; have the frying pan ready and place in it about 2 ounces fresh butter; let it boil; then pour in the eggs and stir quickly until cooked, about 4 minutes, and serve immediately.

47.

EGGS, CURRIED.

Slice 2 onions and fry in butter until brown, add 1 tablespoonful curry powder; add 1 pint of broth made of Extract of Beef, (See No. 3) and stew until onions are tender. Thicken with a little flour or corn starch. Have 8 eggs boiled hard and slice them into the stew. Let them get warm but do not boil.

VEGETABLES.

48.

POTATOES, BAKED.

Potatoes may be baked before the open fire. Have a good bed of coals and place the potatoes on a stone before them. Turn them when necessary. When done they will crack open when squeezed gently in the hand.

49.

POTATOES, BOILED.

The simple operation of boiling potatoes is best performed as follows:—Wash, and leave the skin on, and throw them into boiling water, salted. When soft enough to allow a fork to be thrust through them easily, dash a little cold water into the pot, let the potatoes remain two minutes, and then pour off the water. Replace them over a slow fire until the steam is evaporated. Peel them and place them in an open dish. Time, about half an hour.

50.

POTATOES (RAW), FRIED.

Peel large potatoes and cut in slices a quarter of an inch thick. Dry in a cloth and fry in lard. Have a quick fire, and move the slices of potato continually, turning as required. When crisp, place on a plate to drain, and sprinkle with salt and pepper.

51.

POTATOES, BOILED, TO FRY.

Take any cold potatoes, cut them into slices, and place them in the hot frying pan with plenty of fat. Add salt and pepper, and stir and turn frequently with a knife. Time, about 20 minutes.

52.

POTATO FRITTERS.

Beat together 1 cupful mashed potatoes, 2 eggs (beaten,) 1-2 pint of milk, 1 tablespoonful of flour, (mixed with some of the milk) and a little melted butter, about one tablespoonful. Fry in some lard. Turn when required.

53.

ONIONS, BOILED.

Peel and wash the onions, and boil in salted water until soft. Change the water once, when the onions are half cooked, if so wished. When soft remove from pot, and pour some drawn butter over them (See No. 79.) Time, about half an hour.

54.

ONIONS FRIED.

The following method gives a dish of rather strong onions, but is liked by many. It may be used also to prepare the onions for ham or pork (See 39): Peel and slice the desired number of onions, and place them in the hot frying pan with plenty of lard or pork fat. Add salt, pepper, and sauce, to suit the taste. Stir frequently, and cut as fine as desired while frying. When nearly done sprinkle a little flour over them, and stir them well up so as to cook the flour well, and break all lumps.

55.

VEGETABLES, MISCELLANEOUS.

To cook other vegetables, such as carrots, turnips, etc., to use alone, clean them well, slice them, and lay in cold water until placing them in the pot. Have the water boiling briskly, and salted. Skim the water before putting in the vegetables. When the vegetables sink, they are generally done. Test with a fork, and take them off as soon as done.

56.

CANNED VEGETABLES.

Directions for use generally accompany each can. Canned Tomatoes are especially to be recommended to the hunter, and are excellent when stewed with bread crumbs, or broken biscuit, salt and pepper.

MISCELLANEOUS DISHES.

57.

RICE, PLAIN BOILED.

Pick over the rice and wash it in cold water. To 1 pint rice put 3 quarts of boiling water and 1-2 teaspoonful salt. Boil for 17 minutes from the time it begins to boil. Then pour off all the water, and replace pot over a moderate fire, with cover off, to steam fifteen minutes. Be accurate as to time.

58.

RICE, BOILED, WITH RAISINS.

Prepare the rice as directed in No. 57. When it has been boiled for 10 minutes, throw in a handful of cooking raisins and let boil and steam as in No. 57. If the raisins are put in at first they are liable to be boiled to pieces.

59.

SAVORY RICE.

Wash and pick 1-2 pound rice; stew it gently in a little broth, (made of Ext. Beef,

See No. 3) with an onion, some mixed herbs, and a pinch of salt. When the rice is swelled, dip it out of pan and place before the fire to dry. Then place on a dish and pour the broth it was boiled in round it.

60.

RICE CROQUETTES.

To some cold boiled rice add enough beaten egg to allow of making the rice into balls. Add also sugar and lemon peel, or any flavoring to suit the taste. Then form the mass into small oval balls or cakes, sprinkle with bread crumbs, and dip in beaten egg. Fry in butter. When done sprinkle with sugar.

61.

RICE PUDDING.

See No. 73.

62.

OATMEAL PANCAKES.

Mix together, dry, 1-2 pint flour, 1-2 pint oatmeal, and 2 teaspoonfuls Baking Powder.

Add enough cold water to form into a thick batter, and a pinch of salt. Have the frying pan hot, and grease it with a piece of pork fat. Pour on some of the batter, forming three cakes which will not touch one another. When one side is cooked, turn with a knife. A little experience will teach the exact amount of Baking Powder to use to produce light cakes, and the proper consistency of the batter. A good bed of hot coals is required, to fry properly, and the pan must be well greased before cooking each batch of cakes.

63.

FLOUR PANCAKES.

To 1 pint of flour add enough milk to form into a thick batter. Beat up 3 eggs, and add. Beat the whole until perfectly smooth. Add a pinch of salt. Fry in the frying pan, observing the directions given in No. 62.

64.

INDIAN MEAL CAKES.

(The following is quoted from "The Complete American Trapper," and may be tried if wished. We have never tested this Recipe, but it should be a success.)

"Indian meal cakes are easily made by dropping a quantity of the hot mush (Indian meal porridge, boiled for an hour,) in the frying pan, having previously stirred in a small quantity of soda, (or baking powder) and turning it as soon as the lower side is browned." See directions for frying in No. 62.

65.

OATMEAL PORRIDGE.

Moisten 1 pint of oatmeal with some cold water, add a little salt, and pour into 2 pints of boiling water. Boil half an hour or more. If too thick add more water. Boil slowly and stir frequently.

66.

CORN MEAL PORRIDGE.

Corn, or Indian meal porridge is made in the same manner as Oatmeal, (See No. 65) and the same proportions of meal and water are used. Boil for at least one hour.

67.

CORN MEAL PORRIDGE, FRIED.

The porridge, or *sapaun*, as the Indians term it, produced by following recipe No. 66, may be sliced when cold, and fried with lard or pork fat.

68.

HOE CAKE.

Pour enough boiling water, or milk, on corn meal, (salted) to moisten it. Let it stand for an hour, or longer. Put three tablespoonfuls on the hot frying pan, and form into a round cake about half an inch thick. When brown, turn it over. Grease the pan with lard or pork fat.

69.

CORN BREAD.

Into 1 pint of corn meal pour boiling water enough to wet it. Dissolve one-half teaspoon soda in hot water, (or mix same quantity of baking powder with the meal while dry) and add it with two well beaten eggs, 1 teaspoon salt, and butter the size of an egg. Stir well and bake in buttered pans (tin plates will do) for half an hour in the Dutch oven, or before the open fire. Have a strong fire, in either case.

70.

OAT CAKE.

To 1 pint of oatmeal add 1 teaspoon of baking powder, mix well, and add enough cold water to moisten, and a pint of salt. Spread about half an inch thick on the frying pan well greased. Hold over the fire to bake. Turn when bottom is done; or roast in the Dutch oven. The cake should not scorch, but gradually dry through.

71.

BREAD.

When camping out, we can make excellent bread by the following method :— To 1 quart of flour add 3 teaspoonfuls of baking powder, and mix well while dry. Add a pinch of salt. Mix with cold water, or sweet milk, into a thick dough that can be handled without sticking. Knead it thoroughly; on this depends its excellence. Rub dry flour on the hands to prevent the dough from sticking. Form into round biscuits or loaves. Bake before a good fire, or in the Dutch oven. These biscuits may also be baked in a frying pan, holding it over the fire, to cook slowly, and turning the biscuits as often as necessary. They are best when cold.

PUDDINGS.

72.

BATTER PUDDING, BAKED OR BOILED.

Take 6 ozs. flour, a little salt, and 3 eggs beaten; beat all together with milk, added by degrees, until of the thickness of cream. put into a buttered pan, and bake in Dutch oven for about an hour. If to be boilled, Put the mixture into a buttered and floured mold, (tin cups will answer the purpose) and tie over with a cloth. Place the mould in a kettle of boiling water. Boil one hour and a half, or more. The longer time will produce a lighter article. Eat with butter and sugar.

73.

RICE PUDDING.

Boil some rice and raisins, as directed in No. 58, but do not steam the rice. Let there be a little water in it. When done, add two or three beaten eggs, well stirred in, and a little sugar. Let simmer four or five minutes, and set aside to cool.

74.

COSSACKS' PLUM PUDDING.

Mix well together 1 lb. of flour, 3-4 lb. raisins, 3-4 lb. pork fat chopped fine, 2 tablespoonfuls syrup or sugar, and 1-2 pint water. Tie tightly in a cloth, and boil 4 hours. For sauce see No. 82.

SALAD-DRESSINGS AND SAUCES.

75.

DRESSING FOR CANNED LOBSTER, ETC.

Rub the yolks of 2 hard-boiled eggs to a smooth paste with 1 dessert spoonful of salad oil, or melted butter, add to it 2 teaspoonfuls of made mustard, and 1 teaspoonful fine white sugar, and put to it gradually a cup of vinegar.

Another: —

2 potatoes mashed; 1 tablespoonful made mustard; 1 teaspoonful salt; 3 tablespoonfuls salad oil, or melted butter; 4 tablespoonfuls vinegar; yolks of 2 hard-boiled eggs pounded fine; 1 onion cut fine, and one tablespoonful Anchory or other sauce. Mix all together and pour over lobster, etc.

76.

TOMATO SALAD.

Cut tomatoes, not over ripe, into slices. Cut up, as fine as possible, some small onions, one to each tomato, and sprinkle over slices of tomato. Add pepper, salt and vinegar. Onions may be soaked, or partially cooked, if considered too strong.

77.

DUTCH SAUCE FOR MEAT OR FISH.

Put 6 spoonfuls of water, and 4 of vinegar, into a warm pan, and thicken with the beaten yolks of 2 eggs. Make quite hot, but do not boil. Squeeze in some lemon juice. Pour over meat, etc.

78.

SAUCE FOR DUCKS, GEESE, ETC.

Chop very fine 1 oz. onion and 1-2 oz. sage or mixed herbs. Put them into the frying pan to stew with 4 tablespoonfuls of water. Simmer gently for 10 minutes, then add 1 teaspoonful of pepper and salt, and 1 oz. fine bread crumbs, or biscuit broken very fine. Mix well together. Then pour to it a gill of broth (see No. 3) or melted butter, Stir well together, and simmer a few minutes longer.

79.

DRAWN BUTTER, OR WHITE SAUCE, FOR FISH, ONIONS, ETC.

To the desired quantity of milk, add enough moistened flour to thicken; add a lump of butter and a little salt. Boil slowly for ten or fifteen minutes. If milk cannot be had, water will do. (See 81.)

80.

PUDDING SAUCE.

1 teaspoonful of milk, and 2 yolks of eggs well beaten, and some sugar; place on fire, and stir till it just comes to the boil; then let it cool. When luke-warm, stir it into a

glass of sherry, or the same quantity of water with a small dash of any liquor.

81.

SAUCE HOLLANDAISE, OR DRAWN BUTTER FOR FISH.

2 spoonfuls of flour mixed with 1 pint of water. Place in fry-pan, and when cooked add pepper, salt, lemon juice, and the yolks of 2 eggs, beaten. Take off fire and add 1-2 lb. butter. Stir all the time.

82.

PLUM PUDDING SAUCE.

Mix some fine white sugar with some melted butter; add a glass of sherry, a small glass of brandy, and a little nutmeg and lemon-peel grated.

BEVERAGES.

TEA.

General Remarks.

To ensure having a good cup of tea, you must buy a good article from a responsible grocer. No article of commerce is more largely adulterated, or with more disgusting, baneful substances than tea. The vast difference in the prices of this article shows at once that the modern trade therein has become greatly prostituted. If the tea which is sold for fifteen cents per pound is *good*, how shall we name that which is sold for ninety cents per pound? If the ninety cents is an honest price, and no fancy figure, then the tea sold at the lower price must indeed be trash. That the hunter may be careful when purchasing this his favorite beverage, I quote the following remarks from one of our daily papers: —

"A recent analysis of some samples of alleged tea in New York, showed that the specimens examined contained the following articles: Nutgalls, currant leaves, iron filings, filbert husks, sulphate of copper, oak bark, hornets' and wasps' nests shredded and colored, acetic acid, aloes, manila paper, vernal grass, and other things too numerous and disgusting to mention." As teas vary somewhat in strength, and as different people have different tastes to be suited, it is impossible to lay down any exact rule for the amount of tea to add to a given quantity of water. As a general guide the following formula may be used:—

83.

TEA, TO STEEP OR DRAW.

An old rule runs, "1 teaspoonful for each cup, and one for the tea-pot." This is rather ambiguous. It may mean either "1 teaspoonful for each cup placed on the table, i. e., for each person," or "1 teaspoonful for each cup of tea expected to be used, or for each cup of water placed in the tea-kettle." However, the following is generally used at the camp fire:— Put 1 oz. tea, or 2 1-2 tablespoonfuls, heaped, to 4 pints of boiling water. Remove immediately from the fire. Cover slowly. Shake the kettle, and place by the fire, but do not let it boil. Should this proportion make the tea too strong, or too weak, regulate the next drawing accordingly. Use the purest soft water abtainable.

Tea which is allowed to stand for a long time with the leaves in it, becomes very unwholesome, and if it is desired to keep some cold, to drink during the day, it should be poured from the leaves into another can as soon as sufficiently drawn, or the leaves may be dipped out with a spoon. Tea drank to excess will produce nervousness, and strong green tea may so far injure health as to produce lameness and neuralgia.

84.

COFFEE, TO DRAW.

(Buy fresh ground, rather than the imported packages.)

Add coffee to boiling water in the proportion of 1 oz., or 3 tablespoonfuls, to 1 quart. Boil for 30 minutes or longer. If the coffee does not settle, dash in half a cup of cold water, and let stand a few minutes. Should the coffee be weak, use more when next making.

85.

COFFEE, TO IMPROVE FLAVOR OF

The flavor of coffee may be greatly improved, and its delicate aroma increased, by adding a little soda to the water with which it is made. A very little will suffice.

86.

COFFEE, SUBSTITUTE FOR CREAM IN.

Beat an egg to a froth, put to it a piece of butter the size of a walnut, place in a can and pour the coffee on to it gradually from the pot, or stir the egg into the coffee, when off the fire, if you have no other can at hand.

87.

COFFEE, ESSENCE, OR EXTRACT OF.

This article, sold by grocers, is to be recommended, and produces, with boiling water, an instantaneous cup of coffee. Directions accompany each bottle.

MISCELLANEOUS BEVERAGES.

The following articles, which are all to be recommended, have directions printed on the wrappers or boxes:—Cocoa, chocolate, Cadbury's essence of cocoa, broma, kacka, etc. Cocoa forms a very nourishing drink to partake of in the morning before the labor of cooking a regular breakfast is undertaken, and will be of use to those amateurs who are unaccustomed to very early rising, or to working before breakfast. It may be prepared with water alone, if no milk is to be procured. A few bottles of lime juice will be an excellent addition to the hunter's outfit.

APPENDIX.

The following useful Receipts were omitted under the heading of "Fish":

89.

COD-FISH, SALT, TO BOIL.

Wash the fish well, and cut into pieces, according to size of pot. Place in the pot with cold water and set on fire to boil slowly. Change the water once. This will freshen the fish, and render it cleaner. A good method is to soak the fish, cut up, in water over night, and cook next day. When done, remove skin and bones. For sauce see Nos. 79–81.

90.

FISH CAKES (WITH RAW FISH).

1 pint salt cod-fish, raw, picked very fine, and as many raw, whole, peeled potatoes as will be equal to 2 pints. Put together in cold water and boil until potatoes are thoroughly cooked; remove from the fire and drain off the water. Mash together. Add butter size of an egg, two well-beaten eggs, and a little pepper. Mix well together. Drop, 1 spoonful at a time, into the frying pan well greased with lard. Brown and turn. Do not mould these cakes with the hand; drop the mixture from a spoon. Use sauce, mustard, etc.

91.

FISH CAKES (WITH COOKED FISH).

Take cold, boiled cod-fish and cold, boiled potatoes. Pick all the bones from fish, and mash fish and potatoes together. Add a little pepper, and salt if necessary. Form into cakes, and fry with lard until the outsides are brown and crisp. Use sauce, mustard, etc.

SECTION IX.

THE LAST RESOURCE, OR WHAT TO USE WHEN PROVISIONS RUN SHORT.

The hunter may sometimes find himself far from home, with his provisions at a very low ebb, no money in his pocket, and no game to be secured. It is then that he has to call up all his powers of endurance, and to exercise all his knowledge of cooking to make his provisions go as far as possible. True, if he is passing through a settled country he can not starve, but if his route lies through a land of famine he may have to eat many things which are not included in the list of his ordinary food. We do not generally eat frogs, meadow-hens, or beavers, and yet these are all good articles ot food, and the hunter who can obtain them, when his provisions are expended, should consider himself to be in luck. He might be reduced to the necessity of eating still more objectionable articles. I have known men who were glad to eat skunk flesh. What we eat is more a matter of custom than of the superior fitness of the articles of our diet. This fact appears more fully when we remember that the natives of the South Seas eat their snakes, beetles and worms; the Chinese their birds' nests; the civilized inhabitants of Europe their frogs and horse flesh, and the Esquimaux the oily blubber of the whale. Mostly every school-boy in America can relate how the Indians of the North and West eat their dogs; how the cannibals of Polynesia devour their own species. But we will not enter into any deep discussion on this subject. We merely wish to show the amateur hunter that should he be placed on short rations, by any unavoidable circumstances, or be perfectly destitute of his ordinary food, he has still at his command many articles which will sustain life. The hunter should watch his decreasing stock of provisions with a jealous eye, and so regulate his return journey that he will reach a place where he may replenish his larder before his stock is entirely consumed. As stated elsewhere, the soup-pot is the best utensil to use when rations run short. A proper manipulation will make a small amount of food do great service.

The following receipts may be of use to the hunter; some of them, indeed, may be used at any time, but they are so appropriate for use in times of scarcity of provisions that we have placed them under this head.

92.

POTATO SOUP.

Peel and chop 4 onions and put them into a kettle with 2 oz. fat or butter, add 3 quarts of water, and boil half an hour. Then add 4 lbs. peeled and sliced potatoes, pepper and salt to taste; stir well on the fire for half an hour. Any scraps of meat, biscuits, or a little rice, barley or flour, or some mixed herbs will of course improve this dish.

93.

DANDELIONS, AS GREENS.

Gather some tops of dandelions, wash well, and put into just enough salted boiling water to cover them. When tender squeeze out all the water, place them in the frying-pan, and fry for a few minutes, with a little salt, pepper and butter, or pork fat. When done, add some slices of hard-boiled eggs if obtainable.

94.

CORN MEAL.

If a good supply of this wholesome article is carried in a bag, it will form a valuable stand-by when what is generally considered to be more dainty food is scarce. Methods for using are given in Nos. 64–66–67–68–69.

95.

FROGS, TO ROAST, FRY OR STEW.

The hind legs only of frogs are used. These may be roasted before the fire, (see No. 20,) fried in the pan, (see Nos. 24-25,) or stewed, (see Nos. 23-26,) using such ingredients as are obtainable.

96.

MISCELLANEOUS ARTICLES TO USE.

The following articles may be used if occasion arises: — Squirrels are very good as food. This fact is not generally known among amateur hunters. Cook as directed in Nos. 22 or 25. Meadow-hen; roast, (see No. 22,) fry, (see No. 24) or stew, (see No. 23.) Black-birds — same as meadow-hens. If the hunter has to eat any very strong, objectionable flesh or fowls, the articles should be thoroughly washed and par-boiled, and such things as onions, pepper and salt used freely, if on hand.

INDEX TO SECTION XI.

MISCELLANEOUS RECEIPTS.

	Page.
To preserve Meat and Fish	131
To salt Meat and Fish	132
To preserve Dead Game	133
Boot Grease	133
How to Load a Gun	134

SECTION X.

THE TREATMENT OF DROWNING, WOUNDS, ACCIDENTS, BITES AND STINGS, ETC.

As the hunter is much exposed to accidents, he should have in his outfit such simple remedies as experience teaches him may be most useful. We may enumerate the following articles:—A strip of Sticking Plaster, Bottle of Tincture of Arnica, Bottle of some strong Liniment, Bottle of Diarrhœa Mixture, Bottle of Dark Brandy, and a box of Cathartic Pills.

The following methods of treating Bites, Wounds, Cuts, etc., will prove to be effectual, in the absence of a Physician.

1.

BURNS AND SCALDS.

To burns apply some cotton dipped in oil, or grease the spot with any fat at hand. Scalds may be treated in the same way; or covered with scraped raw potato; or cover the scald with treacle, and dust well with flour.

2.

ORDINARY CUTS.

Use thin strips of sticking plaster. Bring the edges of the wound carefully together.

3.

LARGE CUTS.

Cut two broad pieces of sticking plaster so as to look like a comb; clean the wound, pouring on some lukewarm water; place a piece of the plaster on either side of the wound. These pieces should have been so cut, and must be so arranged, that they shall interlace each other. Cross the projecting strips, or teeth, and by pulling them through each other close the wound, then press the sticking plaster well down, both on the flesh and where it crosses itself.

4.

CONTUSIONS, OR BRUISES.

Bathe with Tincture of Arnica, and bind with a piece of cotton, on which pour a few drops of the Tincture, or bathe in cold water and bind with damp cotton. If the skin is broken dilute the Arnica with twelve parts water.

5.

HEMORRHAGE.

When an artery is divided or torn the blood *jumps* out of the wound, and is of a bright scarlet color. If a vein is injured the blood is darker and flows evenly. To stop the latter apply a bandage, and under it place a piece of cotton or other cloth folded, so as to press on the vein. In applying bandages to arrest arterial bleeding be careful to place them between the wound and the heart. If the wound is in the arm, tie a piece of tape, or cord that will not cut, loosely round the arm above the cut. Pass a small stick under the tape and twist it round until the tape compresses the arm tightly enough to arrest the bleeding. Then tie the stick in position. If it still bleeds place a cork, or piece of wood rolled in cloth, underneath the tape, on the inside of the fleshy part of the arm where the artery may be felt beating. If the wound is in the leg and the twisted tape, placed above the wound, fails to arrest the bleeding, place the cork in the direction of a line drawn from the inner part of the knee a little to the outside of the groin. The object is to compress the artery.

6.

BLEEDING AT THE NOSE.

Plug the nostrils with lint, and bathe the forehead and nose with cold water, keeping the head raised. Raise the arms, and place both hands behind the head, allowing the head to rest on them. To chew a piece of paper, or other substances, also tends to arrest the bleeding.

7.

VIOLENT SHOCKS.

When a person is rendered unconscious, untie all strings, collar, etc., and loosen any clothing that is tight and interferes with the breathing. Raise the head, and note if there is any bleeding from any part; apply smelling salts or a burning feather to the nose, and hot bottles to the feet.

8.

CHOKING.

If a bone, or other substance is caught in the throat, insert the forefinger and press upon the roof of the tongue to induce vomiting. If this does not have the desired effect, swallow a large piece of potato or soft bread. If these fail to remove the obstruction, take a mustard emetic. (A large teaspoonful of mustard, mixed with a tumbler of warm water.)

9.

DROWNING.

Send for medical assistance immediately, and in the mean time proceed as follows: 1. Strip the body and rub it dry; then rub with hot blankets, and place on a warm bed, in a warm room if possible. 2. Cleanse away the froth from the nose and mouth. 3. Apply warm bricks or stones, bottles, etc., to the arm-pits, between the thighs, and to the soles of the feet. 4. Rub the body with the hands enclosed in warm socks. 5. If possible, place the body in a warm bath. 6. To restore breathing, put the pipe of a common bellows into one nostril, (or blow into the nostril) carefully closing the other and the mouth; at the same time draw downwards, and push gently backwards the upper part of the windpipe, to allow a free admission of air; blow the bellows gently, to inflate the lungs, till the breast is raised a little; then set the mouth and nostrils free, and press gently on the chest. Repeat this operation of inflating the lungs until signs of life appear. When the patient revives apply smelling salts to the nose, if obtainable, and give some warm wine or brandy and water. Never hold the body up by the feet. Do not rub the body with salt or spirits and do not roll on casks. These remedies should be continued for twelve hours.

10.

SUNSTROKE, APOPLEXY, AND FITS.

Raise the head and support it by gentle pressure on the sides of the head; unloose all tight clothes, strings, etc., and apply cold water to the head and face. Send for medical assistance if procurable.

11.

NARCOTIC POISONS.

(Bane berries; fools parsley; deadly nightshade; water hemlock; thorn apple; opium, etc.)

Give emetics, large draughts of fluids, tickle the throat, apply smelling salts to the nose, dash cold water over the face and chest, apply mustard poultices, and endeavor to rouse the person by walking between two persons, and, if possible, by electricity.

12.

VEGETABLE IRRITATING POISONS.

(Mezereon; monks-hood; bitter apple; gamboge, etc.)

Give emetics of mustard or chamomile, large draughts of warm milk, or other bland fluids, leech the belly if necessary, and give strong infusion of coffee.

13.

POISONOUS FISH.

(Old-wife; sea-lobster; mussel; tunney; blower; rock-fish, etc.)

Give an emetic, excite vomiting by tickling

the throat, and draughts of warm water. Follow emetics by purgatives, and give sugar and water to drink freely.

14.

BITES OF REPTILES.

(Viper; black-viper; rattle-snake, etc.)

If possible, immediately tie a tape or string between the wound and the heart, and draw tight. Scarify the parts with a penknife, or other sharp instrument to excite bleeding, and apply a cupping glass over the bite, frequently removing it, and bathing the wounds in volatile alkali, (or some liniment.) If a cupping glass cannot be procured, make the wound bleed as much as possible, and suck it, or burn it well with a hot poker. Give the patient plenty of whiskey, if possible, and cover up warmly.

15.

BITES OF MAD ANIMALS.

Tie a string tightly above the part, cut out the bite, and cauterize the wound with a red hot poker. or lunar caustic. Give a purgative, and plenty of warm drink.

16.

SIMPLE BITES.

For small bites (where the animal is not mad) bathe the part well with Tincture of Arnica diluted with twelve times the quantity of water.

17.

NETTLE STING.

Rub the part with green sage leaves, or bathe with water in which some herbs have been steeped.

18.

STINGS OF BEES AND WASPS.

Pull the sting out, pressing a watch key over it to expose it well; suck the wound, if possible, and bathe with cold water.

19.

TREATMENT OF DIARRHŒA.

This complaint is very liable to attack amateur hunters, being induced by change of water, diet, and mode of living. A bottle of Diarrhœa mixture may be procured of any druggist, and should have a place in the hunter's outfit. In absence of such medicine try the following:—Half a cupful of milk or water, and one teaspoonful of pepper, mix and drink. Abstain from soft food. Brandy and pepper is a more effectual remedy. Dr. Franklin, in his "Advice to Swimmers," says: "It is certain that much swimming is the means of stopping diarrhœa, and even of producing constipation. With respect to those who do not know how to swim, or who are affected with diarrhœa at a season which does not permit them to use that exercise. a warm bath, by cleansing and purifying the skin, is found very salutary, and often affects a radical cure."

20.

BLACK-FLIES, MOSQUITOES, ETC., OINTMENTS FOR PROTECTION FROM.

These pests generally infest every locality frequented by the hunter, and to guard against their bites some of the following preparations should be carried:

1. The simple herb, pennyroyal, found in most sandy localities, rubbed on the hands and face, will check the attacks of insects.

2. Make an ointment of 1 ounce oil of pennyroyal, 3 ounces lard. Put into a little wooden box, or wide-mouthed bottle, and apply when required.

3. Mix common tar and sweet oil in equal parts. Bottle for use.

4. Tobacco smoke is obnoxious to mosquitoes, and if the pipe be lighted, those pests will not be so troublesome.

21.

BLACK-FLIES, MOSQUITOES, ETC., TO RID THE TENT OF.

When these insects infest the tent, a smudge should be lighted in the windward doorway or placed under the windward curtain. The smudge is composed of birch, or other bark, set on fire and covered with green grass, leaves, or other materials which will create a large amount of smoke. While the smoke is passing through the tent, drive out all the insects with a towel or cloth, then close the tent, and the smudge may be removed. It is a good plan to continue the smudge outside the tent, in such a position that the breeze will drift the smoke on the canvas. This will drive off the insects without filling the tent with the smoke.

INDEX TO SECTION X.

THE TREATMENT OF DROWNING, WOUNDS, ETC.

No.		Page.
	General Remarks	117
1.	Burns and Scalds	117
2.	Cuts, ordinary	118
3.	Cuts, serious	118
4.	Contusions or bruises	119
5.	Hemorrhage	119
6.	Bleeding at the nose	120
7.	Violent Shocks	121
8.	Choking	121
9.	Drowning	122
10.	Sunstroke, Apoplexy, and Fits	123
11.	Narcotic Poisons	124
12.	Vegetable Irritating Poisons	124
13.	Poisonous Fish	124
14.	Bites of Reptiles	125
15.	Bites of Mad Animals	125
16.	Simple Bites	126
17.	Nettle Sting	126
18.	Stings of Bees and Wasps	126
19.	Treatment of Diarrhœa	126
20.	Black-flies, Mosquitos, etc., Ointments for protection from	127
21.	Black-flies, Mosquitos, etc., to rid the tent of	128

SECTION XI.

MISCELLANEOUS RECEIPTS.

TO PRESERVE MEAT AND FISH.

The hunter may at times secure more game than he can immediately use, and he should then employ some of the following methods to preserve the surplus for future needs:—

1. To dry meat and fish:—For meat, cut the flesh into small, thin strips, all the meat being cleaned off the bones. If venison, place the pieces of meat on the inside of the hide of the animal, and mix well with salt. Roll these pieces up in the hide and let it stand for three hours. Build a frame over the fire-place by driving four forked poles into the ground in the form of a square, and about six feet apart. The forks

should be about four feet above the ground. On these lay a frame-work of poles, spread the strips of meat on the frame, and start a good steady fire of hard wood beneath. Keep the fire lighted for twenty-four hours. The meat thus prepared will keep for almost any length of time. Moose and bear meat is dried in the same manner. If the hide is not available to wrap the salted strips in, place them in layers in any vessel. The object is to let them absorb the salt, which the fire afterward dries in.

Fish may be dried in the same manner. Scale them, spread open by cutting down the back, clean them, and remove backbone.

2 To salt meat and fish:—When it is not desired to keep the meat or fish for any length of time, we may cut the meat into convenient pieces, and place in layers in an earthen vessel, using pepper and salt freely, and keeping the vessel covered in a cool place. For fish, clean as usual, from the belly cut down the back, and so divide into

two pieces, place in layers in an earthen or wooden vessel, sprinkling each piece freely with salt and a little pepper. Keep in a cool place.

TO PRESERVE DEAD GAME.

If only for a short time, clean, pluck and place in a covered jar, using salt and pepper freely. If for a long time, proceed as follows:—Take out the intestines, pluck, fill the inside with unground wheat, and place the fowl in a heap or cask of the same grain, in such a manner as to insure its being covered. It will keep for months.

BOOT GREASE.

A simple preparation for boots and shoes is made as follows: Melt together 1 part black rosin, 2 parts beeswax, and 3 parts tallow (candle will do) or other fat. This keeps the leather soft and waterproof. Pour into a tin box, and melt at fire when wanted to apply.

HOW TO LOAD A GUN.

The following old-fashioned rhyme contains some good hints on loading a muzzle loader :—

"Our sport almost at hand, we charge the Gun,

Whilst ev'ry well-bred Dog lies quietly down.

Charge not before. If over night the piece

Stands loaded, In the Morn the Prime will hiss;

Nor Prime too full, else You will surely blame

The hanging Fire, and lose the pointed Aim

Yet cleanse the Touch-hole first; a Partridge Wing,

Most to the field for this wise Purpose bring.

In charging next, good Workmen never fail

To ram the Powder well, but not the Ball.

SECTION XII.

SIGNS OF THE WEATHER.

It is very convenient for the hunter to be able to tell, by observing the present state of the weather, what state will exist during the next day, or for perhaps a longer period. He may thus tell whether he will be able to strike tent, or start on any arranged excursion on the morrow, or whether he had better remain in camp and avoid a wetting.

The *signs* of the weather, as seen in the sky and clouds, are nothing more than the *existing state* of the weather, but as one state is invariably followed by another of a description which never varies, we may, by observing the present state, after some experience, foretell the state which shall necessarily succeed. In presenting a few remarks to guide the hunter in fore-casting the weather, we shall not touch upon any of the complex considerations by which "the weather prophet" arrives at his learned conclusions. We shall confine ourselves to some of the simplest rules laid down by those observers of nature who have given us the benefit of their studies; rules which have been proved to be trustworthy.

I.

SIGNS IN THE SKY AND HEAVENLY BODIES.

An easily-remembered little rhyme runs as follows:

> Evening red and morning grey
> Will set the traveler on his way;
> But evening grey and morning red
> Will bring down rain upon his head.

This is truth and poetry combined. An old couplet, worthy of credence, says:

> If it rains before seven,
> It will clear before eleven,

In other language, early morning rains do not continue for any length of time.

A clear sky and dead calm at sunset, with the sun going down a well-defined form, but on which the eye can gaze without being dazzled, indicate, in summer, a warm, bright morrow; in winter, such a sunset is succeeded by sharp frost.

A yellow sunset indicates wet, soon to follow.

If it rains before sunrise, there will be a fine afternoon.

A red evening foretells fine weather, but if the color spreads very far upwards from the horizon in the evening; or if the color spreads in like manner at sunrise, it foretells wind or rain, or both.

If the sun at rising appears enlarged there will shortly be sudden and sharp showers, if in summer; but in winter settled and moderate weather.

Halos, cornæ, etc., indicate coming rain or snow.

A haziness in the atmosphere, which obscures the sunlight, and makes the sun look white or ill-defined, foretells rain. If at night the moon and stars grow dim, rain will follow.

If the sun is white at setting, or shorn of his rays, or goes down behind a bank of clouds on the horizon, bad weather is to be expected.

If the moon looks pale and dim, expect rain, if red, wind; if of her natural color, with a clear sky, fair weather will obtain.

If the sun at rising is surrounded by an iris, or circle of white clouds, fair weather will follow, for a short time.

If there are red clouds in the west at sunset, it will be fine; if they have a tint of purple, it will be very fine; or if red, bordered with black in the southeast.

If there be a ring or halo round the sun in bad weather, fine weather is at hand.

If there be lightning without thunder after a clear day, fair weather will continue.

Before much rain the clouds grow bigger, and increase very fast. When the clouds are formed like fleeces, but dense in the middle and bright towards the edges, with a bright sky, they are signs of frost, with hail, snow, or rain. If clouds from high in the air, in thin white trains like locks of wool they foretell wind and probably rain. When a general cloudiness covers the sky, and small black fragments of clouds fly underneath, they are a sure sign of rain, and probably it will be lasting. Two currents of clouds always portend rain, and, in summer, thunder.

If at sunrise many clouds are seen in the west and soon disappear, fine weather will obtain.

If the clouds at sunrise move to the west, fine weather, of short duration, will exist.

If there be a rainbow during continued wet weather, the rain will soon be over.

If a rainbow disappear suddenly, it will be fine.

The following signs all foretell foul, wet weather :—

If the sun rise pale, or purple red, or

even dark blue, there will be rain during the day.

If the clouds are red at sunrise, there will be rain the next day.

If at sunrise many dark clouds are seen in the west, and remain, it will rain on that day.

If the sun at rising is covered by a dark spotted cloud, it will rain the same day.

If the sun burn more than usual, or there be a halo round the sun or moon during fine weather, foul weather is at hand.*

If it rain during sunshine, showers will continue.

If the full moon rise pale; *wet.* If it rise red; *wind*.

If the stars appear larger, and closer, and flicker, rain or wind is at hand.

An Aurora Borealis foretells wet weather.

A continued rain from the south is scarcely

---

* In "The Wreck of the Hesperus" the Old Sailor says:
"I pray thee put into yonder port, For I fear a hurricane."
"Last night the moon had a golden ring, and to night no moon we see."

ever succeeded by settled weather before the wind changes, either to the west or some point of the north.

If rain falls during an east wind, it may be expected to continue for twenty-four hours.

If the sun be seen double, or more times reflected in the clouds, expect a heavy storm.

A very red eastern sky at sunset, indicates bad weather.

2.

SIGNS IN FOGS AND MISTS.

A less complicated class of Signs of the Weather than those observed in the sky, but one none the less accurate in its readings, is that presented by the movements of fogs and mists, and the various circumstances under which these are formed. Some of the simplest conditions under this Class, and the results to which they lead, are as follows:—

If mists rise in low ground and soon vanish, expect fine weather.

If mists rise to the hill-tops, expect rain in a day or two.

A black mist indicates coming wet.

When the fog leaves the mountains and rises higher, fair weather is at hand.

If the dew lies plentifully on the grass after a fine day, it is a sign of another. If not, and there is no wind, rain will follow.

If near the full moon there be a general mist before sunrise, it will be fine for several days.

If the fields are covered with a mist before sunrise, fine weather is indicated.

If a white mist, or dew, form in the eveing near a river, and spread over the adjoining land, there will be fair weather.

If there be a damp fog or mist, with wind, rain will follow.

If the fields in the morning be covered with a heavy wet fog, it will generally rain within two or three days.

If a morning fog form into clouds, at different heights, which increase in size and drive in layers, thunder and heavy rain are foretold.

SIGNS GIVEN BY ANIMALS, INSECTS, AND INANIMATE OBJECTS.

Any change in the weather has its effect upon animals, birds, insects, and some inanimate objects, and these, by their actions, impart to us their knowledge of what state of weather is approaching. True, by observing the signs which have been treated of in Parts 1 and 2 of this Section, we may foretell the coming state as soon as can animals or birds, but by knowing the meaning of the signs which those creatures exhibit, we may avail ourselves of a large store of knowledge which, though second-hand, is ready-made, and as useful as easy of acquirement. The facts which have been noted by Naturalists, etc., under this head, are very volumnious, but we shall refer only to those which may be of use to the hunter.

When rain is coming, ravens caw, swallows chatter, small birds plume themselves and make a show of washing, crows make a great noise in the evening, and geese cackle more than usual.

Sheep huddle together at the approach of

bad weather, and turn their tails in its direction. Dogs feel lazy at the approach of rain.

If spiders, in spinning their webs, make the terminating filaments long, we may, in proportion to their length, conclude that the weather will be fine and continue so for ten or twelve days. Spiders generally alter their webs once in 24 hours; if they do this between six and seven in the evening, there will be a fine night; if they alter their web in the morning, a fine day; if they work during rain, expect fine weather, and the more active and busy the spider is, the finer will be the weather. If spiders web (gossamer) fly in the autumn with a south wind, expect an east wind and fine weather. When spiders break and destroy their nests, and creep away, wet weather may be expected.

If gnats fly in compact bodies in the beams of the setting sun, there will be fine weather.

If bats flutter and beetles fly about, there will be a fine morrow.

If owls scream during foul weather, it will change to fair.

If storks and cranes fly high and steadily, fair weather.

In all of the following cases, rain is to be expected:

If ditches and drains smell stronger than usual.

If tobacco smoke seems denser and more powerful.

If the convolonlus and chickweed close.

If foxes and dogs howl and bark more than usual.

If moles cast up hills.

If horses stretch out their necks, and sniff the air, and assemble in the corner of a field, with their heads to leeward.

If turkeys gobble, and if quails make more noise than usual.

If sea-birds fly towards land, and land-birds to sea.

If swallows fly lower than usual.

If the crow makes a great deal of noise, and fly round and round.

If water-fowl screams more than usual, and plunge into the water.

If cranes place their bills under their wings.

If fish bite more readily, and gambol near the surface of the streams and ponds.

If frogs and toads croak more than usual.

If the owl screech.

When sea-gulls and other birds fly inland a storm is to be expected.

If the wind be hushed with sudden heat, thunder and rain are foretold.

General Remarks.

Sudden rains do not last long, but when the air grows thick by degrees, and the sun, moon, and stars shine dimmer and dimmer, it is then likely to rain six hours.

After very warm and calm weather, a squall or storm, with some rain, may follow; likewise at any time when the atmosphere is heated much above the usual temperature of the season, and when there is, or recently has been, much electric or magnetic disturbances in the atmosphere.

Storms are most frequent in December, January and February. In September there are generally one or two storms. The vernal equinoctial gales are stronger than the autumnal.

NOTE. All mention of the readings of scientific instruments as presaging the weather, has been purposely omitted, as the general hunter does not carry such instruments on his excursions. While it is impossible to enumerate the sources whence the remarks on the weather have been gathered, I wish, nevertheless, to express my indebtedness to a very useful volume entitled "Enquire Within," and to a copy of "Venner's Almanac."

FINIS.

"In less than one hundred pages is much and deep philosophy."

THE STARS AND THE EARTH;

OR

Thoughts upon Space, Time and Eternity.

WITH AN INTRODUCTION BY

THOMAS HILL, D.D., L.L.D.
Late President of Harvard University.

Cloth, 50 Cents.

"The main purpose of the book is to show, from the laws of light, how the past may be actually present to God, and may hereafter become actually present to men."— *Churchman, New York.*

"The author takes up the phenomenon of light, and by it shows how the past is the present with God. Further on, he seeks to prove the unity of the Creator by the proofs of unity pervading the creation, laying down the theory that the universe may be the embodiment of a single thought occupying neither space nor time. The volume is sublime poetry "— *Christian Register, Boston.*

"It is poetic in its suggestions, and leaves the impression that nature gives the cue to things hidden and mysterious. There is no dogmatic conclusion, and yet the dogmas of omnipresence and omniscience are elucidated by it. In less than one hundred pages is much and deep philosophy "— *Boston Commonwealth.*

"It cannot but be valuable to the student of science as well as the professor of religion, and tends to bring them closer together and reconcile them "— *Potter's Monthly.*

"We commend the book to the curious and thoughtful reader, assuring him that having once read it he will not be likely ever to forget the impressions made by it "— *Chicago Advance.*

SHORTHAND WITHOUT A MASTER.

UNIVERSAL PHONOGRAPHY;
OR
SHORTHAND BY THE "ALLEN METHOD."

A Self-Instructor, whereby more Speed than Long-Hand Writing is gained at the First Lesson, and additional Speed at each subsequent Lesson.

By G. G. ALLEN,
Principal of the Allen Stenographic Institute, Boston.

Price 50 Cents.

There is scarcely any acquirement so helpful to the student, scientist, or professional man, as shorthand writing. Heretofore, all the methods have required so long a time before one could become so proficient as to make it of any advantage, that men in middle life or busy men have not been able to give the time to learn it; but by the "Allen Method" one can most in "the idle moments of a busy life," certainly, in an hour a day two or three months, become so expert as to report a lecture verbatim.

m Rev. Dr. THOMAS HILL, *Late President of Harvard College.*

PORTLAND, June 2, 1883.

most cordially indorse the main principles of Mr. Allen's method of presenting phonography; they all are thoroughly practical, and must, of necessity, lead to better practical results than the analytic methods usually pursued. I hope Mr. Allen's methods will bring into more general use the phonographic style of shorthand.

From R. M. PULSIFER, *of* R. M. PULSIFER & Co., *Proprietors of the "Boston Herald."*

THE "HERALD," BOSTON, Aug. 17, 1881.

Dear Sir:—I have for the past eight months employed as my private stenographer a gentleman educated at your Institute, and recommended to me by you. I have been entirely satisfied with the service which he has rendered. Respectfully yours, R. M. PULSIFER.

37 MATTHEWS, HARVARD COLLEGE.

I had taken but two lessons of you, and at my third lesson I wrote three times as fast as an ordinary long-hand writer.

S. B. PEARMAIN.

164 HANOVER STREET, BOSTON.

After taking a two months' course I wrote from matter with which I was entirely unfamiliar, one hundred and forty words per minute.

B. C. STICKNEY.

549 THIRD STREET, BOSTON.

Before completing a three months' course I could write one hundred and sixty-five words per minute. I find no difficulty in taking down sermons, speeches, lectures, etc., verbatim. THOMAS F. MACKEY

I have taken a **three months'** course of lessons, and am now doing law reporting. MINNIE E. CONLAN.

Reporting for some of the best Boston lawyers, she earns more in a day than ordinary lady employés can in a week.

How the Ant can be enlarged to the size of the Elephant.

BEGINNINGS WITH THE MICROSCOPE.
A WORKING HANDBOOK,

Containing Simple Instructions in the Art and Method of Using the Microscope, and Preparing Articles for Examination.

By WALTER P. MANTON, M.D.,

Author of "Taxidermy without a Teacher," "Insects," and "Field Botany."

Illustrated, Price 50 Cents.

This dainty little manual treats of

1. The Microscope and Working Tools.
2. Preparing Objects.
3. Stains and Staining.
4. Embedding.
5. Needle Preparations and Section Cutting.
6. Mounting.
7. How to Work.
9. What to work with.

Dr. Manton, whose previous "Practical Helps to Natural History" are having an extensive sale, here gives in a simple and comprehensive manner, a fund of information about "the revealer of those particles which in the aggregate go to make up bodies visible to the naked eye, but which, taken singly, are so small that their size must be magnified many times in order that the human eye may determine their structure."

This handbook will be found equally valuable as a manual for schools, as an instructor to the energetic youth who receives one of these valuable instruments as a premium, or as a book of reference by the lucky youngster who has a sample deposited in his Christmas stocking or left beside his place on his birthday.

HANDBOOK OF THE TELEPHONE.

☞ EVERYBODY WANTS

THE TELEPHONE.

AN ACCOUNT OF THE

Phenomena of Electricity, Magnetism, and Sound, as involved in its action; with directions for making a Speaking Telephone.

BY

Prof. A. E. DOLBEAR, of Tufts College.

Author of "THE ART OF PROJECTING."

16mo. Illustrated. 50 Cents.

———•◦•———

"An interesting little book upon this most fascinating subject, which is treated in a very clear and methodical way. First, we have a thorough review of the discoveries in electricity, then of magnetism, then of those in the study of sound—pitch, velocity, timbre, tone, resonance, sympathetic vibrations, etc. From these the telephone is reached and by them in a measure explained."—*Hartford Courant.*

"It treats of electricity, magnets, the galvanic battery, thermo-electricity, magneto-electricity, magnetic induction, and all the appliances for producing the wonderful and useful results that have already come to the world by the invention of the telephone. It is a little book that will be desired by all classes of the community; neatly printed and tastefully bound. Every young person in the land should become familiar with the principles of physical science involved in this discovery."—*N.E. Journal of Education.*

"This is a subject of much interest at present, and Prof. DOLBEAR'S exposition of it will be welcomed. The author elucidates the phenomena of electricity, magnetism and sound, as involved in the action of the telephone; describes the workings of the speaking telephone, and gives directions for making one. The author is specially qualified to write on the subject, as he is the inventor of the telephone which he describes. His descriptions are plain and are helped out by a dozen or more engravings."—*Boston Journal.*

"No little book is capable of doing better service."

ELOCUTION SIMPLIFIED.

By WALTER K. FOBES.

WITH AN INTRODUCTION BY GEORGE M. BAKER.

Cloth, 50 Cents.

"The Manual is divided into four parts. Part First describes a series of gymnastics to give strength and elasticity to the muscles used in speaking. Part Second is a system of vocal exercises for daily practice. Part Third, the application of the vocal exercises to the reading of short extracts, showing the effect when thus applied. Part Four is a chapter giving general hints on elocution, and showing how easily defects in speech may be cured.

With or without an instructor, this Manual is just what the student is in great need of and he can supply that need by a study of 'Elocution Simplified.'" — *The Dartmouth, Hanover, N.H.*

"A very useful book for boys, giving them practical instruction in an art altogether too much neglected now in our educational methods." — *Hartford Courant.*

"This valuable little book occupies a place heretofore left vacant, as a digest of elocution that is both practical and methodical, and low in price." — *N. Y. Tribune.*

"No little book is capable of doing better service in the community, if its inculcations and instructions are carefully followed." — *The Churchman, New York.*

"A book treating this subject within a limited space, and bringing it within the comprehension of the novice and amateur of the art, is certainly needed. We believe that this is just such a work." — *The Normal Teacher.*

"The rules laid down are explicit and to the point, and are illustrated by copious extracts from the great masters of English speech. The Appendix contains some valuable hints on lisping, stammering, stuttering, and other defects of speech." — *Commercial Bulletin, Boston.*

"Mr. Geo. M. Baker has written an interesting introduction, full of valuable advice." — *Boston Gazette.*

A MOST VALUABLE COMPANION.

FIELD BOTANY:

A Hand-Book for the Collector.

CONTAINING

Instructions for Gathering and Preserving Plants, and the Formation of a Herbarium; also, Complete Instructions in Leaf Photography, Plant Printing, and the Skeletonizing of Leaves.

By WALTER P. MANTON.

Illustrated.   Cloth, 50 Cents.

"A most valuable companion   The amount of information conveyed in the small compass is surprising."— *Demorest's Monthly*, *New York*.

"It is just what the boys and girls need for the spring campaign in Botany, and at the modest price of fifty cents is accessible to all."— *Christian Register*, *Boston*.

"It is entirely practical, and gives the collector just the knowledge required to render his work permanent and satisfactory   Its smallness fits it to be carried in the pocket, which is a consideration."— *National Baptist*, *N.Y.*

"Of inestimable value to young botanists."— *Rural New Yorker*.

"There are many practical suggestions in the book, also, which would probably be new, and which would certainly be useful to teacher as well as pupil."— *Kingston (N.Y.) Freeman*.

"We heard a class of bright young botanists recite the other day, and we thought at the time how delightful a thing it would be to prosecute in these blossoming months that entertaining study ourselves.   Perhaps we shall carry out the thought   If we do, this little work shall be our *vade mecum*." - *Chicago Standard*.

THE TRIBULATIONS OF A FRENCHMAN.

BROKEN ENGLISH.

A Frenchman's Struggles with the English Language.

Amusing as a narrative, instructive as a handbook of French conversation.

BY PROF. E. C. DUBOIS,

Author of "The French Teacher, a right system of teaching French."

Cloth, 50 cents; cheap edition, paper, 30 cents.

Who has not heard of Professor Dubois, "the funny Frenchman"? Many will remember his instructive, amusing, and witty lectures, "Broken English; or, the Mistakes, Trials, and Tribulations of a Frenchman while wrestling with the English Tongue." After listening to his story of how he went to the theatre expecting to see Laura Keene appear in two pieces, supported by her husband; how he told some of his mishaps over and over again, because his hearers kept saying "Do tell," "I want to know," &c.; how he said, "kicked the bucket," and used other expressions of a like nature, supposing them to be the most polite forms of speech; what a struggle he had with certain little words to find out how to say broken off, broken up, broken out, broken down, broken in, &c., and how he made other mistakes almost without number, many a listener has expressed the hope the Professor would have the lecture put in some permanent form, that it might not be forgotten.

Finally taking the advice of his friends, Professor Dubois has concluded to add the materials collected in later years, and have the whole published as one of Lee and Shepard's popular handbooks.

It is published in English and French, on opposite pages, and will thus be a very valuable aid to those learning French.

"FULL OF SERVICEABLE INFORMATION."

HANDBOOK OF CONVERSATION:

Its Faults and Its Graces.

COMPRISING

1. Dr. Peabody's Lecture.   2.—Mr. Trench's Lecture.
3.—Mr. Parry Gwinn's "A Word to the Wise; or, Hints on the Current Improprieties of Expression in Writing and Speaking."
4.—Mistakes and Improprieties in Speaking and Writing Corrected.

COMPILED BY

ANDREW P. PEABODY, D.D., L.L.D.,
Late of Harvard University.

Cloth, 50 Cents.

"A book which will be of incalculable value to the young man or woman who will carefully note and follow out its numerous and valuable suggestions. It is worth owning, and ought to be studied by many who heedlessly misuse their mother tongue."—*Boston Beacon.*

"This little manual contains a great variety of valuable matter for the instruction of those who would improve their style in conversation. It is in fact one of the very best and clearest handbooks of its kind that we have seen."—*The Day, Baltimore.*

"It is a useful hand book on the proprieties and common errors of English speech."—*The Churchman.*

"The book is full of serviceable information and can be advantageously read and kept for reference by every one who desires to converse and to write properly and gracefully."—*Paper World.*

"Here is a neat pocket-volume, which every person should have for ready reference. For the young it is of especial value and to the old it is of great interest."—*Vox Populi.*

KNOW WHAT YOU ARE DRINKING.

WATER ANALYSIS:

A Handbook for Water Drinkers.

BY G. L. AUSTIN, M. D.

Price 50 Cents.

"This little book furnishes to non-professional men a ready and pleasing method of determining water to the extent necessary to afford a perfect idea as regards its wholesomeness for drinking purposes. We cannot but congratulate the author on the happy conception and execution of this work, which cannot fail to make many friends in its behalf."— *Chicago Chemical Review.*

"The tests are, for the most part, simple, and are described in language devoid of technicalities. The work will be of service to all who wish to know what they are drinking."— *Medical Bulletin, Phila.*

"This will prove a very acceptable book to those who drink water, and who have any special desire to know what kind of water they drink. It has been prepared by an entirely competent person."— *Chicago Interior.*

"It condenses into fifty pages what one would have to wander through a small chemical library to find. We commend the book as deserving of a wide circulation."— *N. Y. Independent.*

"Another of Lee and Shepard's model little 'Handbooks,' which have proven a popular card. It contains the gist of the science."— *Des Moines State Leader.*

"A most valuable little book."— *Boston Globe.*

"Dr. Austin is a well-known authority, and his conclusions will command attention."— *Brooklyn Eagle.*

"No one can peruse this book, even for a few moments, without seeing that it is very systematic and concise; plainly written, and well worth the price asked."— *Medical and Surgical Journal, St. Louis.*

USEFUL IN AN EMERGENCY.

WHAT IS TO BE DONE?

A Handbook for the Nursery, with useful Hints for Children and Adults.

By ROBERT B. DIXON, M.D.

SURGEON OF THE FIFTH MASS. INFANTRY;

PHYSICIAN TO THE BOSTON DISPENSARY.

Price, cloth, 50 cents; paper, 30 cents.

This is not only a useful, but at the same time a clever little handbook, and one which is well adapted for all who have any regard for their own health or that of their children. The book contains hints and remedies for the treatment of accidents and diseases, and they are so clearly arranged that any one can easily understand what do do in an emergency when a physician cannot be reached, or before his services can be obtained. Besides the general hints, there is a prefix containing a set of rules on the personal care of the health, arranged in such a clear and concise manner that they will be not only instructive, but, at the same time, exceedingly interesting reading. If people of all classes cannot or will not eat, drink, and avoid all that is recommended in this book, at least they can learn the reason why such and such conditions of atmosphere, diet, and exercise should be sought for, and such and such determining causes of ill health be shunned. If every boy and girl in the land could be taught the rules to be found in this little book, we have no hesitation in saying they would be saved much suffering and disease, and would add incalculably to the strength of our Continent by producing and preserving a sounder and more vigorous race of human beings.

This handbook will be found especially useful for cottagers during the summer season, who live at some distance from their physician.

It is, without doubt, the best book of the kind yet prepared for the non-professional world.

THE MOST COMPLETE BOOK OF THE KIND EVER WRITTEN.

PRACTICAL BOAT-SAILING.

A concise and simple Treatise on the Management of Small Boats and Yachts under all Conditions; with Explanatory Chapters on ordinary Sea Manœuvres, and the Use of Sails, Helm, and Anchor, and Advice as to what is proper to be done in Different Emergencies; Supplemented by a short

VOCABULARY OF NAUTICAL TERMS.

By DOUGLAS FRAZAR,

Formerly Fourth Officer of the Steamship "Atlantic," Master of the Bark "Maryland," and Commander of the Yacht "Fennimore Cooper" in the Northern Seas of China and Japan.

Numerous Illustrations.   Cloth, $1.00.

"Capt. Frazar has done his work in a sailorly way, using no technicalities but which he explains fully before he goes an inch further. His ideas are clear and concise, his method simple and practical, and his teachings so plain that his little book will be hailed with real pleasure by all who are embryo yachtsmen. The illustrations, of which there are over two dozen, are 'right to the point,' and from them the beginner can at once 'see' what some men would take pages to explain. * * This little work is of great practical value, and should be in the hands of every yachtsman."— *Nautical Gazette.*

"Capt. Frazar is the son of a shipmaster, and was familiar with boats, Yachts, and shipping generally, from his youth until he rose to the top of his profession as a seaman. * * It is, unquestionably, the most complete book of the kind ever written, and will, no doubt, be read with interest by all who have anything to do with boats or yachts."— *Traveller, Boston.*

"Its directions are so plain, that with the aid of the accompanying pictorial illustrations and diagrams given in the book, it does seem as if 'anybody,' after reading it, could safely handle a sailboat in a squall."— *Times, Hartford.*

"The work is admirably done, and by a thorough study of these directions, boat sailing, which has been considered the most dangerous, is really made one of the most safe of sports."— *Providence Journal.*

"Of course Capt. Frazer does not pretend that one may become an expert sailor by reading his book, but he gives a great amount of valuable information, and so smooths the way to the practical knowledge which can only be gained by actual experience."— *New Bedford Mercury.*

"Here is a book that every boy ought to have. There are certain things boys *will* do. They fish, shoot, swim, and sail It may be added that they also drown and are shot. * * Boys should be taught how to do these things which, when ignorantly attempted, yield danger. Here we have a good guide to the art of boat sailing; sensible instruction, full explanation, and a clear evidence of the fact that to be careless is to be in danger. We can heartily commend the volume."— *Hartford Courant.*

"JUST HOW IT IS DONE."

WHIRLWINDS, CYCLONES, AND TORNADOES.

By Prof. W. N. DAVIS.
(Harvard College.)

Cloth, 50 cents.

"A popular treatise upon the causes of these phenomena, which have lately become of such frequency in the West and South, has become much needed. The public have become somewhat familiar with these through reading of their terrible effects, but there is a too general lack of knowledge as to their causes. The study of the natural phenomena of the earth, sea, and air have yielded great additions to the general stock of knowledge on these subjects, and the reasons giving rise to any one of these great disturbances, as well as the more common experiences of rain and wind, can be accurately explained, if not always predicted, by those who watch the weather reports. Every one should master the explanations given in this little book." — *Lowell Times.*

"Any of the thousands in this country who have been blown into the middle of next week by tornadoes during the past few years can discover precisely how it was done by reading this little book, which belongs to Lee & Shepard's 'Science Series.' It is in fact an essay on the theory of storms, accompanied by a number of cuts and diagrams intended to throw additional light upon the subject. To say the very least of the book, it is exceedingly interesting and instructive, whether the theory advanced is correct or not." — *Chicago Herald.*

"Mr. Davis, who is an instructor in Harvard College, in the essay before us, has given his theory of storms, in an interesting and convincing manner. At a time like the present, when the West seems singled out for the most extraordinary natural disturbances, and the East is not free from dangerous storms and floods, such a work is of real value, not only as showing the causes, but also the means of prevention, of those apparently ungovernable phenomena. The action of whirlwinds and cyclones, the causes of motion, the danger of tornadoes, etc., are clearly described, and are useful to the scientist as well as to the layman." — *Boston Commercial Bulletin.*

www.ingramcontent.com/pod-product-compliance
Lightning Source LLC
Chambersburg PA
CBHW030305170426
43202CB00009B/882